· TROPHIES ·
Intervention
ASSESSMENT BOOK
Grade 4

Harcourt

Orlando   Boston   Dallas   Chicago   San Diego

Visit *The Learning Site!*
www.harcourtschool.com

ISBN 0-15-326157-9

7 8 9 10   170   10 09 08 07 06 05 04

Introduction

The *Intervention Assessment Book* is an assessment tool for making instructional decisions. The skills that are assessed are the ones that are reinforced in the *Intervention Reader* selections. For each lesson in the *Intervention Teacher's Guide,* there is a phonics assessment and a selection comprehension assessment.

Each phonics assessment consists of 8 multiple-choice items that require students to discriminate phonic elements among words and fill in answer circles. This assessment may be used independently or in conjunction with the selection comprehension tests that follow.

The selection comprehension assessment was designed to measure students' reading comprehension of the main selections featured in the *Intervention Readers.* Each two-page test consists of ten questions that assess understanding of selection content and vocabulary. The first eight questions are multiple-choice items requiring students to fill in answer circles. The remaining two questions are constructed-response items requiring students to write words, phrases, or sentences.

Administering

When the phonics assessment is administered, tell students that they will need to fill in the correct answer circle for each item. Explain that they will need to decode each answer choice before choosing the correct answer. If necessary clarify directions or items students don't understand. Allow enough time for all students to complete the assessment, although most students should be able to complete a single test in under thirty minutes.

Prior to administering the comprehension assessment, tell students they are going to be answering questions about the selection they have just read. They will need to fill in the correct answer circles for the first eight multiple-choice items and to write short answers for the last two items. These directions are also printed on the tests. If necessary, clarify directions or questions that students don't understand, as long as the clarification does not reveal any answers. Allow enough time for all students to complete the assessment, although most students should be able to complete a single test in under an hour.

Scoring

Answer Keys

Mark multiple-choice questions as either correct or incorrect, using the Answer Keys. For the constructed-response items, students' responses may not exactly match provided answers. Be sure to allow credit for student responses that *reflect* those provided in the Answer Keys. Because measuring comprehension—not writing skills—is the primary objective of this assessment, do not deduct points for spelling, writing mechanics, or language conventions.

Student Record Forms

Use the Student Record Forms to record and track a student's performance. It is important to consider student performance on the tests as only one of the many tools and strategies that might be used to provide a comprehensive picture of achievement. The sum of all formal and informal assessment information becomes a reliable source for measuring student progress and for affecting instructional change. Use students' scores and responses, in addition to performance on other assessment tools, daily work samples, and information obtained in student conferences, to determine the need for additional instruction or intervention.

Contents
Grade 4 • *Moving Ahead*

Harcourt • Moving Ahead • Intervention Assessment Book

Name _____ Date _____

Fill in the circle in front of the word that makes sense in the sentence.

1. Six people can ride in Dad's _____ .
- ○ van
- ○ vane
- ○ vat

2. Nate took a trip on a _____ .
- ○ plan
- ○ plane
- ○ plant

3. Please put the pictures in a new _____ .
- ○ fan
- ○ fame
- ○ frame

4. Our marching band led the _____ .
- ○ parade
- ○ glade
- ○ amaze

5. A _____ with no plants looks bare.
- ○ landing
- ○ landscape
- ○ language

6. Kate read the book to her _____ .
- ○ classmates
- ○ climates
- ○ classic

7. Our banner is at the top of the _____ .
- ○ flagpole
- ○ flypaper
- ○ flatboat

8. I _____ a cake for the party .
- ○ mad
- ○ mud
- ○ made

Directions: For items 1–8, fill in the circle in front of the correct answer. For items 9–10, write the answer.

1. Where does this story take place?
   Ⓐ in the country
   Ⓑ in a schoolyard
   Ⓒ in the city
   Ⓓ in a vacant vase

2. The main characters in this story are _____ .
   Ⓐ Gram and Blake
   Ⓑ Gram and the man
   Ⓒ Blake and the man
   Ⓓ the firefighter and the man

3. Gram uses all of the following as vases **except** _____ .
   Ⓐ vacant lots
   Ⓑ hats
   Ⓒ a skate
   Ⓓ cake pans

4. In this story, *bulbs* are _____ .
   Ⓐ plant parades
   Ⓑ things that give off light
   Ⓒ pockets filled with dirt
   Ⓓ things from which some plants grow

5. In the story, *in the future* means that something _____ .
   Ⓐ happened a long time age
   Ⓑ happened yesterday
   Ⓒ will happen in time to come
   Ⓓ is happening right now

Harcourt • Moving Ahead • Intervention Assessment Book

6. What happens when Gram and Blake go to the plant parade?

Ⓐ The flowers march around the station.

Ⓑ People are staring at the beautiful flowers.

Ⓒ Gram wants to retire from gardening.

Ⓓ Blake takes the spade and plants more plants.

7. How does Gram feel about drab landscape?

Ⓐ She likes drab landscape.

Ⓑ She wants to spruce it up.

Ⓒ She loves to plant with a spade.

Ⓓ Blake wants to plant, too.

8. One man _____ Gram for sprucing up the corner.

Ⓐ is annoyed with

Ⓑ is pleased with

Ⓒ gives money to

Ⓑ stares at

9. What does Blake learn from Gram?

_____

_____

_____

_____

10. What do you think will happen if Gram spots more vacant land?

_____

_____

_____

_____

Harcourt • Moving Ahead • Intervention Assessment Book

Fill in the circle in front of the word that makes sense in the sentence.

1. Dad will pay the gas _____ .
- ○ ball
- ○ bill
- ○ bale

2. Please put the _____ on the jam jar.
- ○ lid
- ○ lad
- ○ laid

3. My cat can _____ under the bed.
- ○ hid
- ○ had
- ○ hide

4. Our team will _____ the game.
- ○ wane
- ○ won
- ○ win

5. Let's pick the flowers on the _____ .
- ○ landslide
- ○ hillside
- ○ seaside

6. I am _____ to help you.
- ○ willing
- ○ filling
- ○ spilling

7. Open the box and see what is _____ .
- ○ outside
- ○ beside
- ○ inside

8. Milk is _____ out of the glass.
- ○ spilling
- ○ smiling
- ○ spinning

Harcourt • Moving Ahead • Intervention Assessment Book

Click!

Directions: For items 1–8, fill in the circle in front of the correct answer.
For items 9–10, write the answer.

1. Mike likes to _____ .
   Ⓐ take pictures
   Ⓑ make the class smile
   Ⓒ give a fish pin to Miss Wise
   Ⓓ be a kick

2. In her leisure time, Miss Wise _____ .
   Ⓐ teaches school
   Ⓑ raises goldfish
   Ⓒ collects pins
   Ⓓ has disappointments

3. What does Miss Wise want her class to see if they like?
   Ⓐ doing an art project
   Ⓑ becoming collectors
   Ⓒ putting on a play
   Ⓓ selling their collections

4. Tim has a collection of _____ .
   Ⓐ nine hats
   Ⓑ six hats
   Ⓒ airplanes
   Ⓓ stamps

5. What does Mike like best in Jill's collection?
   Ⓐ a red-and-white airplane
   Ⓑ a white stamp with a plane on it
   Ⓒ having Mike take her picture
   Ⓓ five blue pigs

6. Mike thinks Linda's collection might smell because he thinks she collects _____ .

(A) witch wigs

(B) tickling cats

(C) live pigs

(D) black cats

7. In this story, *salutations* are _____ .

(A) difficult situations

(B) answers to math problems

(C) groups of similar objects

(D) greetings

8. Which word best tells about Miss Wise?

(A) mean

(B) fun

(C) stern

(D) boring

9. How does Miss Wise add to Mike's collection?

_____

_____

_____

10. How does the author show without saying it that Mike is saving each person's picture?

_____

_____

_____

Name _____ **Date** _____

Fill in the circle in front of the word that makes sense in the sentence.

1. Todd skidded down the slippery
_____ .

○ slick

○ slap

○ slope

2. Just _____ your head to say
"yes."

○ nod

○ not

○ nose

3. There is a black _____ on my
new sock.

○ spine

○ spot

○ spite

4. I _____ you will visit me again.

○ hop

○ hot

○ hope

5. Jill is _____ her pet cat.

○ strong

○ stroking

○ striving

6. The _____ is a bird that sings.

○ robot

○ robber

○ robin

7. The log in the fireplace is
still _____ .

○ smoking

○ stoking

○ poking

8. Will has been _____ five miles
every day.

○ joking

○ jogging

○ jigging

Harcourt • Moving Ahead • Intervention Assessment Book

Directions: For items 1–8, fill in the circle in front of the correct answer. For items 9–10, write the answer.

1. Where does this story begin?
   - (A) at a school
   - (B) at home
   - (C) in the schoolyard
   - (D) at camp

2. Ron hopes to be in the play, and _____ .
   - (A) he is disappointed
   - (B) he gets the greatest lines
   - (C) his parents are not coming to the pageant
   - (D) he will be a dog in the pageant

3. For the pageant, Ron practices telling jokes because he wants _____ .
   - (A) to make mistakes in the show
   - (B) to know where to stand on stage
   - (C) to say his lines correctly
   - (D) his fake nose to fit

4. What problem does Ron have with the fake nose?
   - (A) It is too big.
   - (B) It is too small.
   - (C) It smells funny.
   - (D) It flops up and down.

5. In the story, *lopes on stage* means _____ onto the stage.
   - (A) sneaks quietly
   - (B) trips
   - (C) walks very sadly
   - (D) runs like a fox

Harcourt • Moving Ahead • Intervention Assessment Book

6. When the nose falls over Ron's mouth, he _____ .

(A) becomes upset and forgets his lines

(B) can't see the audience

(C) puts it on top and grins

(D) hears his mother and father clap

7. How does Ron solve the nose problem?

(A) He doesn't wear the nose.

(B) He puts the nose on his head.

(C) He keeps the nose over his mouth.

(D) He turns around and walks off the stage.

8. In this story, a stage is _____ .

(A) where the actors perform

(B) an old-time wagon

(C) a time in a child's growth

(D) a very big step

9. What is the class's play all about?

_____

_____

_____

_____

10. What is the greatest joke in the pageant?

_____

_____

_____

_____

Fill in the circle in front of the word that makes sense in the sentence.

1. A parrot has a strong _____ .
   - ○ bead
   - ○ bean
   - ○ beak

2. We planted carrot _____ in the garden.
   - ○ seeds
   - ○ seams
   - ○ seals

3. Fish swim in the _____ .
   - ○ stream
   - ○ strike
   - ○ streak

4. Use your _____ to open the door.
   - ○ kite
   - ○ keep
   - ○ key

5. We found _____ on the beach after the storm.
   - ○ seashore
   - ○ seaweed
   - ○ season

6. Ned is _____ his old bike.
   - ○ selling
   - ○ spelling
   - ○ sweeping

7. We are _____ because we are tired.
   - ○ testing
   - ○ jesting
   - ○ resting

8. This street is so long that it seems _____ .
   - ○ hopeless
   - ○ sleepless
   - ○ endless

Harcourt • Moving Ahead • Intervention Assessment Book

Lesson 4: *Joe DiMaggio, One of Baseball's Greatest*

Joe DiMaggio, One of Baseball's Greatest

Directions: For items 1–8, fill in the circle in front of the correct answer. For items 9–10, write the answer.

1. This story is like a biography, because it's _____ .
   - Ⓐ make-believe
   - Ⓑ about someone's life
   - Ⓒ about a lot of facts
   - Ⓓ written by Joe DiMaggio

2. Who was a famous ball player with the Yankees when Joe DiMaggio joined the team?
   - Ⓐ Lou Gehrig
   - Ⓑ Ted Williams
   - Ⓒ Sammy Sosa
   - Ⓓ Michael Jordan

3. At first the Yankee fans did not think Joe DiMaggio would be good for the team, because _____ .
   - Ⓐ he had a bad arm
   - Ⓑ he couldn't hit
   - Ⓒ he had a bad leg
   - Ⓓ he was a show-off

4. In this selection, *tremendous find* means _____ .
   - Ⓐ a lost player
   - Ⓑ a wonderful surprise for the Yankees
   - Ⓒ a player needing a big salary
   - Ⓓ one of the greatest pitchers

5. In this selection, *immigrant* means someone who is born _____ .
   - Ⓐ at home
   - Ⓑ in a different city from where he or she is now living
   - Ⓒ in another country and then moves to the United States
   - Ⓓ in the United States and then moves to another country

6. In 1937 Joe DiMaggio _____ .

   (A) hit the most home runs in baseball

   (B) was not hitting that year

   (C) didn't get up to bat because of his leg

   (D) hit base hits but no homers

7. During the 1941 season, Joe _____ .

   (A) struck out in 20 games

   (B) got a hit in 56 straight games

   (C) got hits in his last 10 games

   (D) did not miss one game

8. In this story, a *manager's* job is _____ .

   (A) to be the first baseman of the Yankees

   (B) to coach first base for the Yankees

   (C) to be in charge of the baseball team

   (D) to train the players

9. Name two facts you learned from this story about Joe DiMaggio.

_____

_____

_____

_____

10. Why did the fans appreciate DiMaggio?

_____

_____

_____

_____

Name _____ **Date** _____

Fill in the circle in front of the word that makes sense in the sentence.

1. I had to _____ the mud from my hands.
   - ○ shrub
   - ○ scrub
   - ○ snub

2. That bee has _____ me!
   - ○ stung
   - ○ strum
   - ○ stamp

3. It's fun to ride in a pick-up _____ .
   - ○ truck
   - ○ track
   - ○ trick

4. That old bike is nothing but _____ .
   - ○ jug
   - ○ junk
   - ○ jump

5. A horse is a very _____ animal.
   - ○ unicorn
   - ○ uniform
   - ○ useful

6. No one can _____ me of being late.
   - ○ use
   - ○ accuse
   - ○ fuse

7. The TV will not work when it is _____ .
   - ○ uncut
   - ○ unstuck
   - ○ unplugged

8. We are _____ the windows to keep out the cold.
   - ○ shutting
   - ○ shouting
   - ○ shining

Harcourt • Moving Ahead • Intervention Assessment Book

Amelia's Flying Lesson

Directions: For items 1–8, fill in the circle in front of the correct answer. For items 9–10, write the answer.

1. What is Amelia like?
- Ⓐ brave and outspoken
- Ⓑ shy and quiet
- Ⓒ not very friendly
- Ⓓ angry

2. June and Amelia are friends, but _____ .
- Ⓐ they are just alike
- Ⓑ they are very different
- Ⓒ they do not play together
- Ⓓ they do not like each other

3. More than anything, Amelia dreams of _____ .
- Ⓐ wearing elegant dresses
- Ⓑ playing games
- Ⓒ driving a car
- Ⓓ flying

4. Why does Amelia want to build a slide?
- Ⓐ so the girls will have a playground
- Ⓑ to show how brave she is
- Ⓒ to go fast and see how it feels to fly
- Ⓓ as a gift for her brother

5. At first, June thinks she and Amelia will _____ on the slide.
- Ⓐ never play
- Ⓑ have fun
- Ⓒ get hurt
- Ⓓ break the apple box

Harcourt • Moving Ahead • Intervention Assessment Book

6. At the end of the story, June _____ .

Ⓐ wants to fly

Ⓑ wants to take down the slide

Ⓒ calls her mother

Ⓓ takes Amelia to the doctor

7. *June marveled at how brave Amelia was* means June _____ .

Ⓐ always knew Amelia was brave

Ⓑ was amazed at how brave Amelia was

Ⓒ asked someone if Amelia was brave

Ⓓ asked Amelia to show that she was brave

8. A *brisk* day is _____ .

Ⓐ very hot

Ⓑ freezing cold

Ⓒ cool and windy

Ⓓ dark and rainy

9. Does Amelia or June change more during the story? Tell how you know.

_____

_____

_____

_____

10. Do you think it was a good idea to build the slide? Explain your answer.

_____

_____

_____

_____

Name _____ **Date** _____

Fill in the circle in front of the word that makes sense in the sentence.

1. My sister likes to shop at the _____ .
   - ◯ wall
   - ◯ hall
   - ◯ mall

2. Mom put a little _____ on the green peas.
   - ◯ salt
   - ◯ halt
   - ◯ malt

3. Some leaves change color in the _____ .
   - ◯ fell
   - ◯ full
   - ◯ fall

4. My brother is as _____ as my dad.
   - ◯ tall
   - ◯ tell
   - ◯ tail

5. The batter hits the _____ with a bat.
   - ◯ basketball
   - ◯ baseball
   - ◯ volleyball

6. Don't ride your bike on the _____ .
   - ◯ sideburns
   - ◯ sidestroke
   - ◯ sidewalk

7. The workers will _____ new phones.
   - ◯ install
   - ◯ inside
   - ◯ insect

8. Loud _____ is not permitted in the library.
   - ◯ taking
   - ◯ talking
   - ◯ ticking

Harcourt • Moving Ahead • Intervention Assessment Book

Can-Do Kid

Directions: For items 1–8, fill in the circle in front of the correct answer. For items 9–10, write the answer.

1. This play takes place _____ .

   Ⓐ at the mall

   Ⓑ outside a stadium

   Ⓒ in a supermarket

   Ⓓ in Walt's yard

2. Walt likes to spend his money on _____ .

   Ⓐ sunglasses

   Ⓑ magazines

   Ⓒ CDs

   Ⓓ tapes

3. Why can't Walt buy the CD he wants right away?

   Ⓐ The CD man doesn't have it.

   Ⓑ Walt already has too many CDs.

   Ⓒ Walt doesn't have ten dollars.

   Ⓓ That CD has not come out yet.

4. The CD man thinks Walt looks like _____ .

   Ⓐ an honest kid

   Ⓑ a shiftless kid

   Ⓒ a kid with a lot of money

   Ⓓ his brother

5. The CD man tells Walt he will _____ .

   Ⓐ sell all his CDs soon

   Ⓑ close early today

   Ⓒ stay open until dark

   Ⓓ keep the CD for Walt until 2:00

6. How does Walt plan to get $5.00?

(A) ask his dad for it

(B) earn it

(C) take it from his savings

(D) borrow it from Duncan

7. In this play, *elated* means _____ .

(A) without money

(B) surprised

(C) thrilled with joy

(D) angry

8. In this play, the CD man speaks *indignantly* when _____ .

(A) he is sad

(B) he is angry because something is not fair

(C) he is enjoying his work

(D) he is feeling sick

9. How does Walt help the CD man's business?

_____

_____

_____

_____

10. Why does the CD man call Walt a can-do kid?

_____

_____

_____

_____

Name _____ **Date** _____

Fill in the circle in front of the word that makes sense in the sentence.

1. The puppy _____ its tail when it is happy.
   - ○ wides
   - ○ wigs
   - ○ wags

2. It may _____ , so take your umbrella.
   - ○ rain
   - ○ run
   - ○ ran

3. Please _____ here just a little longer.
   - ○ stay
   - ○ say
   - ○ stray

4. We hiked up a steep _____ .
   - ○ tray
   - ○ trail
   - ○ train

5. Ms. Gray will _____ our homework.
   - ○ expert
   - ○ explain
   - ○ explode

6. Our class got a $20 _____ for picking up litter.
   - ○ payment
   - ○ pavement
   - ○ painter

7. The _____ runs under the city streets.
   - ○ subject
   - ○ subtract
   - ○ subway

8. The _____ will bring us the hamburgers we ordered.
   - ○ water
   - ○ waiter
   - ○ wetter

**Directions: For items 1–8, fill in the circle in front of the correct answer.
For items 9–10, write the answer.**

1. Ray has given Loyal a _____ home.
   - (A) lonely
   - (B) big and fancy
   - (C) cold
   - (D) warm and loving

2. Loyal likes to chase things, but he _____ .
   - (A) never hurts them
   - (B) always catches them
   - (C) likes to catch fish best
   - (D) always chases big things

3. How does Loyal feel when Ray says he is brave?
   - (A) ashamed
   - (B) important
   - (C) indignant
   - (D) elegant

4. Loyal thinks he must _____ to find out how brave he is.
   - (A) chase something really big
   - (B) stay with Ray all the time
   - (C) leave home
   - (D) hang a name plate

5. _Ray neglected to close the gate_ means _____ .
   - (A) Ray closed the gate as usual.
   - (B) Ray usually didn't close the gate.
   - (C) Ray asked someone else to close the gate.
   - (D) Ray did not close the gate.

Harcourt • Moving Ahead • Intervention Assessment Book

6. In this story, *insignificant* means _____ .

Ⓐ very important

Ⓑ not small

Ⓒ not having a sign

Ⓓ not worth much

7. What job does Frank give Loyal?

Ⓐ to keep his big dog company

Ⓑ to herd sheep

Ⓒ to go for the mail

Ⓓ to keep the fox from getting the hens

8. At the end of the story, Loyal _____ .

Ⓐ lives on the farm

Ⓑ goes back home to Ray

Ⓒ fights with the big dog

Ⓓ makes friends with a fox

9. How does Loyal get hurt?

_____

_____

_____

_____

10. What lesson does Loyal learn in the story?

_____

_____

_____

_____

Fill in the circle in front of the word that makes sense in the sentence.

1. We came to the game to _____ for our team.
- ○ cheer
- ○ chore
- ○ chair

2. Beth walked along the shady _____ .
- ○ pant
- ○ patch
- ○ path

3. In the fairy tale, the rabbit made three _____ .
- ○ washes
- ○ wishes
- ○ watches

4. It is polite to say, "_____ you."
- ○ Think
- ○ Thank
- ○ Than

5. After the rain, the sky was filled with beautiful _____ .
- ○ sunshine
- ○ suntan
- ○ sunstroke

6. I like to have bubbles in my _____ .
- ○ bother
- ○ batter
- ○ bathtub

7. I would like to _____ these skates for smaller ones.
- ○ expire
- ○ exchange
- ○ express

8. The _____ will catch something for his dinner.
- ○ fishpond
- ○ fishing
- ○ fisherman

Harcourt • Moving Ahead • Intervention Assessment Book

Bringing Back the Puffins

Directions: For items 1–8, fill in the circle in front of the correct answer. For items 9–10, write the answer.

1. This story takes place in the _____ .
(A) winter   (B) spring
(C) summer   (D) fall

2. Steve Kress tries to _____ .
(A) keep puffins from nesting at Egg Rock
(B) visit uninhabited Egg Rock
(C) collect puffin chicks
(D) bring puffin chicks to Egg Rock

3. Steve and his team make good parents because they do all the following **but** _____ .
(A) make a town for the chicks
(B) make burrows for nestlings
(C) feed the chicks fresh fish
(D) keep the chicks safe from the gulls

4. Puffins are made for life in the sea because they _____ .
(A) are poor swimmers and divers
(B) catch fish with their webbed feet
(C) can swim fast and dive deep
(D) have sharp beaks

5. What do the puffins do when they come out of their burrows?
(A) make a wobbly flight to the sea
(B) fly around Egg Rock for days
(C) hunt for food and eat
(D) dive right into the sea

6. After the puffins try their wings, they _____ .

Ⓐ catch fish

Ⓑ eat dinner

Ⓒ take a nap

Ⓓ swim away

7. What do the puffins have that helps them fish?

Ⓐ a sharp beak

Ⓑ black feathers

Ⓒ strong wings

Ⓓ long claws

8. At the end of the story, Steve spies a _____ .

Ⓐ bright speck

Ⓑ small airplane

Ⓒ gull

Ⓓ puffin

9. What big hope does Steve Kress have for the puffins?

_____

_____

_____

_____

10. What are two dangers the puffins face at sea?

_____

_____

_____

_____

Harcourt • Moving Ahead • Intervention Assessment Book

Name _____ **Date** _____

Fill in the circle in front of the word that makes sense in the sentence.

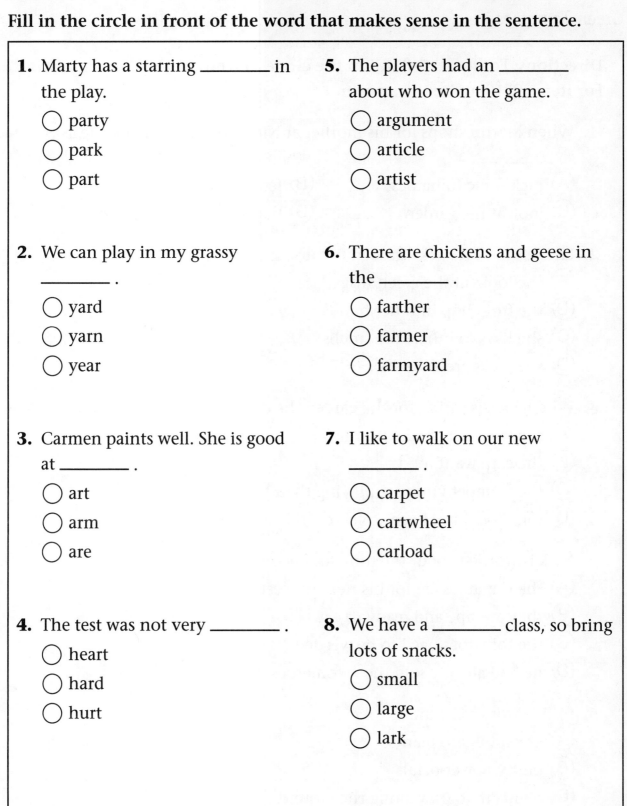

1. Marty has a starring _____ in the play.
- ◯ party
- ◯ park
- ◯ part

2. We can play in my grassy _____ .
- ◯ yard
- ◯ yarn
- ◯ year

3. Carmen paints well. She is good at _____ .
- ◯ art
- ◯ arm
- ◯ are

4. The test was not very _____ .
- ◯ heart
- ◯ hard
- ◯ hurt

5. The players had an _____ about who won the game.
- ◯ argument
- ◯ article
- ◯ artist

6. There are chickens and geese in the _____ .
- ◯ farther
- ◯ farmer
- ◯ farmyard

7. I like to walk on our new _____ .
- ◯ carpet
- ◯ cartwheel
- ◯ carload

8. We have a _____ class, so bring lots of snacks.
- ◯ small
- ◯ large
- ◯ lark

Green Tomatoes

Directions: For items 1–8, fill in the circle in front of the correct answer. For items 9–10, write the answer.

1. When Martin shops for his mother at Nick's vegetable stand, he asks to _____ .
   - (A) pick some tomatoes
   - (B) feed Nick's fish
   - (C) look at the garden
   - (D) buy some green tomatoes

2. Lil likes to visit Nick's garden because _____ .
   - (A) she looks at the green frogs
   - (B) the frogs hop into her hands
   - (C) she likes to inhale the smells
   - (D) she picks green beans

3. When Nick is caring for the garden, he discovers that _____ .
   - (A) the lavender needs trimming
   - (B) the carp want food
   - (C) the trumpet vines are playing their trumpets
   - (D) tomatoes have been stolen off the vines

4. Nick is worried about the tomatoes because _____ .
   - (A) the tomatoes are for his next harvest
   - (B) they are ripe and ready to eat
   - (C) the tomatoes need to be weeded
   - (D) he had already sold those tomatoes

5. In this story, *vines* are _____ .
   - (A) green tomato plants
   - (B) pretty flower petals
   - (C) plants that grow along the ground
   - (D) tall bushes with tomatoes on them

Harcourt • Moving Ahead • Intervention Assessment Book

6. Nick _____ the wall for his mural with a yardstick.

Ⓐ measures

Ⓑ paints

Ⓒ washes

Ⓓ shares

7. Lil's green balls really are _____ .

Ⓐ small plastic balls

Ⓑ Nick's green tomatoes

Ⓒ the balls she likes best

Ⓓ green and yellow pickles

8. Nick *sniffed and blinked* means that he _____ .

Ⓐ started to laugh

Ⓑ smelled something bad

Ⓒ was holding back his tears

Ⓓ got something in his eye

9. Why doesn't Nick take money from Carla for the tomatoes?

_____

_____

_____

_____

10. What does Nick decide he can sell?

_____

_____

_____

_____

Name _____ **Date** _____

Fill in the circle in front of the word that makes sense in the sentence.

1. The rain will _____ my garden and help it grow.
   ○ sock
   ○ soak
   ○ seek

2. May I have jelly on my _____?
   ○ taste
   ○ test
   ○ toast

3. Do you know who _____ this skateboard?
   ○ owns
   ○ oaks
   ○ owes

4. Ms. Kelly, our new _____, teaches us to play ball.
   ○ coal
   ○ coat
   ○ coach

5. A _____ will keep you dry when it's wet outside.
   ○ raindrop
   ○ raincoat
   ○ rainfall

6. In winter it's fun to throw _____.
   ○ snowslides
   ○ snowballs
   ○ snowmen

7. You need to be strong to move a _____ across a lake.
   ○ roadway
   ○ robot
   ○ rowboat

8. It may not be safe to _____ a strange dog.
   ○ approach
   ○ apply
   ○ apron

Harcourt • Moving Ahead • Intervention Assessment Book

A Day with the Orangutans

**Directions: For items 1–8, fill in the circle in front of the correct answer.
For items 9–10, write the answer.**

1. The story takes place _____ .
   - (A) in the desert of Borneo
   - (B) in the rain forest of Borneo
   - (C) on the Mississippi
   - (D) in the zoo

2. Baby orangutans have become endangered for all the following reasons
   but that _____ .
   - (A) the orphans know how to find food
   - (B) some are smuggled out of the forest
   - (C) some are sold as pets
   - (D) when trees are cut, they are in danger

3. The mother orangutan cares for her young for about _____ .
   - (A) one year
   - (B) two years
   - (C) eight years
   - (D) ten years

4. Orangutan mothers sometimes have to deal with bad behavior from
   their young, because orangutans _____ .
   - (A) like to be left alone
   - (B) make faces when they feel like it
   - (C) like people to play with them
   - (D) throw tantrums when they are upset

5. Why are the orangutan's hands specially shaped?
   - (A) so they can get food
   - (B) for washing and grooming themselves
   - (C) so they can grip tree branches and climb trees
   - (D) to play games with their friends

Harcourt • Moving Ahead • Intervention Assessment Book

6. In this selection, *depend* means _____ .

   Ⓐ to take care of an orangutan

   Ⓑ to rely on someone or something

   Ⓒ having to do with people

   Ⓓ to do something over and over again

7. In this selection, an *orphan* is an orangutan that _____ .

   Ⓐ has no parents

   Ⓑ has two sets of parents

   Ⓒ has grandparents

   Ⓓ has no brother or sister

8. The orangutan shows how it's feeling through _____ .

   Ⓐ clapping its hands

   Ⓑ stomping its feet

   Ⓒ making noises

   Ⓓ facial expression

9. Why does the mother orangutan teach her babies how to make a nest?

_____

_____

_____

_____

10. Why do some people want to save the rain forest?

_____

_____

_____

_____

Harcourt • Moving Ahead • Intervention Assessment Book

Name _____ **Date** _____

Fill in the circle in front of the word that makes sense in the sentence.

1. Heavy rain fell during the
   _____ .
   - ○ thorn
   - ○ corn
   - ○ storm

2. The lion made a loud _____ .
   - ○ roar
   - ○ soar
   - ○ board

3. I dropped the vase, and it landed
   on the _____ .
   - ○ floor
   - ○ four
   - ○ forest

4. Trent will _____ himself a glass
   of milk.
   - ○ court
   - ○ pour
   - ○ four

5. You can play this game all by
   _____ .
   - ○ you're
   - ○ yourself
   - ○ yours

6. It is _____ to learn to read.
   - ○ improve
   - ○ impress
   - ○ important

7. We hung a cloth over the
   _____ to our room.
   - ○ doorway
   - ○ freeway
   - ○ parkway

8. Taylor found shells at the
   _____ .
   - ○ underscore
   - ○ seashore
   - ○ before

Directions: For items 1–8, fill in the circle in front of the correct answer. For items 9–10, write the answer.

1. When does this story take place?
   - Ⓐ in the present day
   - Ⓑ ten years ago
   - Ⓒ a long time ago
   - Ⓓ in the future

2. Where does the story take place?
   - Ⓐ in a sod house in Baltimore
   - Ⓑ in a sod house in Oregon
   - Ⓒ by the sea in Maryland
   - Ⓓ on the Oregon Trail

3. In this story, a *quilt* is used as a _____ .
   - Ⓐ blanket on the bed
   - Ⓑ picture on the wall
   - Ⓒ bed covering
   - Ⓓ decoration on the wall

4. What does Patrick do for work?
   - Ⓐ takes portraits
   - Ⓑ puts out fires
   - Ⓒ visits people who live in the country
   - Ⓓ catches snakes

5. Why does Patrick ask the family to pose for their pictures outdoors?
   - Ⓐ The house is too small.
   - Ⓑ The women want to wear their bonnets.
   - Ⓒ The house has too much light inside.
   - Ⓓ Patrick always takes outdoor photos.

Harcourt • Moving Ahead • Intervention Assessment Book

6. How does Kate's mother feel after the fire is put out?

Ⓐ She is very upset.

Ⓑ She thinks they must move to a safer place.

Ⓒ She is thankful the family is safe.

Ⓓ She is afraid there will be another fire.

7. Patrick is a kind person because he _____ .

Ⓐ leaves right after the fire

Ⓑ offers to come back in the fall with the pictures

Ⓒ helps Kate's mother care for the animals

Ⓓ helps Kate's father replant the fields before he leaves

8. Since there is time to replant the crops, the fire must have happened in the _____ .

Ⓐ winter

Ⓑ spring

Ⓒ summer

Ⓓ fall

9. Compare Kate's life out West with the life she had in Baltimore.

_____

_____

_____

10. What does Kate mean when she thinks, "It had not been a perfect day, but it had been a perfect visit"?

_____

_____

_____

Name _____ **Date** _____

Fill in the circle in front of the word that makes sense in the sentence.

1. Have you ever _____ Pearl sing?
   - ○ heard
   - ○ hurry
   - ○ hurt

2. I wish I could spell that _____ .
   - ○ worm
   - ○ world
   - ○ word

3. A _____ is a big help to a doctor.
   - ○ nurse
   - ○ worse
   - ○ verse

4. My soccer uniform got _____ .
   - ○ chirp
   - ○ dirty
   - ○ shirt

5. It was a _____ day for a picnic.
   - ○ prefer
   - ○ perhaps
   - ○ perfect

6. My sister gave me a present for my _____ .
   - ○ birthday
   - ○ Thursday
   - ○ workday

7. The number just before fourteen is _____ .
   - ○ forty
   - ○ thirty
   - ○ thirteen

8. My favorite color is _____ .
   - ○ purpose
   - ○ purple
   - ○ purse

Harcourt • Moving Ahead • Intervention Assessment Book

> **Directions: For items 1–8, fill in the circle in front of the correct answer. For items 9–10, write the answer.**

1. Why does Pearl clean up her room?

   Ⓐ Her sister is going away.

   Ⓑ Her stepsister is visiting for two weeks this summer.

   Ⓒ Pearl is going to visit her stepsister.

   Ⓓ She'll be sharing her room with her new stepsister.

2. In this story, *irritably* means _____ .

   Ⓐ pleasantly

   Ⓑ sadly

   Ⓒ crossly

   Ⓓ loudly

3. In this story, *ignore* means _____ .

   Ⓐ to like someone or something very much

   Ⓑ to not pay attention to someone or something

   Ⓒ something that gives pleasure

   Ⓓ neat or orderly

4. How is LaVerne's hair different from Pearl's?

   Ⓐ LaVerne's hair is long and curly. Pearl's is short and straight.

   Ⓑ LaVerne's hair is short and curly. Pearl's is straight and short.

   Ⓒ LaVerne's hair is straight and long. Pearl's is short and curly.

   Ⓓ They both wear their hair the same way.

5. In this story, Pearl likes _____ .

   Ⓐ math

   Ⓑ sports

   Ⓒ reading

   Ⓓ music

6. Why does Pearl sneak out of the house in the morning?

   Ⓐ She likes being with her friends.

   Ⓑ She doesn't want to be with LaVerne.

   Ⓒ LaVerne wants to be by herself.

   Ⓓ Pearl had a tennis match.

7. Pearl's stepfather predicted that the girls _____ .

   Ⓐ would not like each other

   Ⓑ would like the same TV programs

   Ⓒ would hold a grudge against each other

   Ⓓ would find pastimes they both enjoy

8. What does Pearl do at her school?

   Ⓐ tutors first graders in reading

   Ⓑ coaches first graders in soccer

   Ⓒ tutors first graders in math

   Ⓓ plays on the soccer team

9. What gives Pearl the idea that LaVerne does not like sports? Is she correct?

_____

_____

_____

10. What does LaVerne mean when she says, "I guess parents can be right once in a while"?

_____

_____

_____

Harcourt • Moving Ahead • Intervention Assessment Book

Fill in the circle in front of the word that makes sense in the sentence.

1. Inventors have creative
_____ .

  ○ ideas

  ○ irons

  ○ icing

2. Give your story an interesting
_____ .

  ○ tie

  ○ tiny

  ○ title

3. We saw a covered wagon at the
history _____ .

  ○ mustard

  ○ music

  ○ museum

4. The sun shone in the clear
_____ .

  ○ sly

  ○ sky

  ○ spy

5. Amy _____ came back from
New York.

  ○ richly

  ○ recently

  ○ recorder

6. A _____ is a beetle with a red
back and black spots.

  ○ ladybug

  ○ lakeside

  ○ later

7. Cody put thick slices of _____
on his hamburger.

  ○ together

  ○ tomorrow

  ○ tomato

8. Students prepare for careers at
a _____ .

  ○ uniform

  ○ university

  ○ universe

Directions: For items 1–8, fill in the circle in front of the correct answer. For items 9–10, write the answer.

1. This story takes place at the end of _____ .

   Ⓐ spring

   Ⓑ summer

   Ⓒ fall

   Ⓓ winter

2. Who is the first animal to know that the acorns are ready?

   Ⓐ Bo, the wood rat

   Ⓑ Davis, the jay

   Ⓒ Mavis, the owl

   Ⓓ Ruben, the squirrel

3. When Ruben *eavesdropped,* he _____ .

   Ⓐ listened to treehoppers talking

   Ⓑ followed the treehoppers

   Ⓒ asked the treehoppers about the acorns

   Ⓓ made the acquaintance of wood rats

4. "Davis's *antics* were familiar to Mavis" means that _____ .

   Ⓐ Davis's voice was harsh, not musical

   Ⓑ Davis was a great singer

   Ⓒ Mavis had seen him carry on before

   Ⓓ Mavis wanted to sleep all day long

5. Amy, the deer, wishes for wings so she and her mother can _____ .

   Ⓐ find some leaves to eat

   Ⓑ fly away from the owls

   Ⓒ fly with the other animals

   Ⓓ eat acorns on picnic day

Harcourt • Moving Ahead • Intervention Assessment Book

Name _____ **Date** _____

6. Who are the last animals to hear about picnic day?

    Ⓐ the jays

    Ⓑ the owls

    Ⓒ the deer

    Ⓓ the wood rats

7. Why do the owls skip lunch?

    Ⓐ They're not hungry.

    Ⓑ They are too sleepy.

    Ⓒ They want fish for lunch.

    Ⓓ They like to sing at lunchtime.

8. Acorns are more than a treat. They are good for everything **but** _____ .

    Ⓐ helping animals get ready for winter

    Ⓑ winter food that can be stored

    Ⓒ making homes from the sticks

    Ⓓ tossing around as balls

9. Why do the animals relax when the owls leave the picnic?

_____

_____

_____

_____

10. Why is picnic day such an important event for the animals?

_____

_____

_____

Harcourt • Moving Ahead • Intervention Assessment Book

Name _____ **Date** _____

Fill in the circle in front of the word that makes sense in the sentence.

1. My grandma bakes a tasty cherry
   _____ .
   - ○ tie
   - ○ pie
   - ○ lie

2. My feet hurt because my shoes
   are too _____ .
   - ○ sight
   - ○ right
   - ○ tight

3. The airplane's _____ was a
   little bumpy.
   - ○ flight
   - ○ might
   - ○ slight

4. Ms. Preston will _____ the
   ribbon around the box.
   - ○ tie
   - ○ sigh
   - ○ fly

5. A _____ helps ships get to
   shore safely.
   - ○ lightness
   - ○ lighthouse
   - ○ lightly

6. Cars zip along the new _____ .
   - ○ highlight
   - ○ hideout
   - ○ highway

7. Meeting a grizzly bear would be a
   _____ event.
   - ○ lightning
   - ○ frightening
   - ○ tightening

8. _____ are sometimes called
   lightning bugs.
   - ○ Fireflies
   - ○ Firefighters
   - ○ Fireworks

Lesson 14: A Pen Pal in Vietnam

Directions: For items 1–8, fill in the circle in front of the correct answer. For items 9–10, write the answer.

1. Michelle lives in _____ .
   - (A) Vietnam
   - (B) a city in California
   - (C) a small village in California
   - (D) Ho Chi Minh City

2. Michelle understands Kim's letters because _____ .
   - (A) Michelle speaks the same language that Kim does
   - (B) Kim is Vietnamese, but she writes in English
   - (C) Michelle's neighbor translates the letters
   - (D) Kim writes very clearly

3. Michelle thinks Kim probably _____ .
   - (A) lives in a city
   - (B) eats the same foods she does
   - (C) works on a farm that is very dry
   - (D) helps with the work in the rice fields

4. When Kim goes to the city, she rides in a _____ .
   - (A) canoe
   - (B) rowboat
   - (C) bus
   - (D) car

5. Kim and Michelle both feel _____ when they visit a big city.
   - (A) confident
   - (B) confused
   - (C) scared
   - (D) indignant

6. One difference between the United States and Vietnam is that _____ .

  Ⓐ girls in Vietnam don't wear shorts

  Ⓑ girls in Vietnam wear bamboo hats all the time

  Ⓒ women in Vietnam never wear hats

  Ⓓ Vietnam has no large cities

7. If a food is *appetizing,* it _____ .

  Ⓐ smells very bad

  Ⓑ looks as if it would taste good

  Ⓒ doesn't look familiar

  Ⓓ is very hot

8. Another word for *occasionally* is _____ .

  Ⓐ often

  Ⓑ never

  Ⓒ every night

  Ⓓ sometimes

9. Name three things mentioned in the selection that are the same in Vietnam and the United States.

_____

_____

_____

10. Describe Michelle's plans for her trip to Vietnam. Be specific.

_____

_____

_____

_____

Harcourt • Moving Ahead • Intervention Assessment Book

Name _____ **Date** _____

Fill in the circle in front of the word that makes sense in the sentence.

1. A big drum makes a _____ sound.
   - ○ plowed
   - ○ loud
   - ○ crowd

2. A big river has the _____ to flood a town.
   - ○ tower
   - ○ flower
   - ○ power

3. The king wore a golden _____ on his head.
   - ○ crown
   - ○ crowd
   - ○ count

4. I _____ a penny under my desk.
   - ○ fanned
   - ○ fund
   - ○ found

5. I try not to color _____ the lines of the picture.
   - ○ outside
   - ○ outdoors
   - ○ outfield

6. _____ work hard on a ranch.
   - ○ Cowbells
   - ○ Cowards
   - ○ Cowboys

7. I'm busy, but I'll get the work done _____ .
   - ○ something
   - ○ somehow
   - ○ summer

8. Moles travel in _____ tunnels.
   - ○ underway
   - ○ underground
   - ○ understand

Wolf Pack: Sounds and Signals

Directions: For items 1–8, fill in the circle in front of the correct answer. For items 9–10, write the answer.

1. Wolves live _____ .
   - (A) alone
   - (B) in pairs
   - (C) in packs
   - (D) in schools

2. One way that one wolf talks to another is by _____ .
   - (A) meowing
   - (B) howling
   - (C) singing
   - (D) making its own sound

3. A mother wolf will _____ when she talks to her pups.
   - (A) bark
   - (B) growl
   - (C) howl
   - (D) squeak

4. The leader of the wolf pack is the _____ wolf.
   - (A) alpha
   - (B) beta
   - (C) chief
   - (D) king

5. The alpha wolves use all the following signals **except** _____ .
   - (A) holding their tails in the air
   - (B) staring at another wolf
   - (C) laying a paw on another wolf
   - (D) biting and fighting with another wolf

Harcourt • Moving Ahead • Intervention Assessment Book

6. The setting of this selection is the _____ .

Ⓐ forest

Ⓑ tundra

Ⓒ mountains

Ⓓ ocean

7. Baby wolves are called _____ .

Ⓐ kittens

Ⓑ dogs

Ⓒ pups

Ⓓ cubs

8. In this selection, *cooperation* means _____ .

Ⓐ working together

Ⓑ fighting with someone

Ⓒ communicating with others

Ⓓ excitement

9. Name at least one way that members of a pack tell each other they want to be friends.

_____

_____

_____

_____

10. Give an example of how one wolf communicates with another wolf.

_____

_____

_____

Fill in the circle in front of the word that makes sense in the sentence.

1. A dime is worth ten _____ .
   - ○ center
   - ○ sends
   - ○ cents

2. Our costumes have _____ decorations on the sleeves.
   - ○ family
   - ○ fancy
   - ○ fantasy

3. I can't _____ which book to read next.
   - ○ delight
   - ○ divide
   - ○ decide

4. My little brother rides his _____ on the sidewalk.
   - ○ tricycle
   - ○ trickster
   - ○ trimmer

5. I had _____ and milk for breakfast.
   - ○ serious
   - ○ cereal
   - ○ city

6. We should settle our arguments _____ .
   - ○ peak
   - ○ peach
   - ○ peacefully

7. Let's have a party to _____ the beginning of school.
   - ○ celery
   - ○ celebrate
   - ○ cellar

8. Our team will _____ win the game tomorrow.
   - ○ certainly
   - ○ circle
   - ○ circus

Harcourt • Moving Ahead • Intervention Assessment Book

Who Invented This?

Directions: For items 1–8, fill in the circle in front of the correct answer. For items 9–10, write the answer.

1. An invention is _____ .

   Ⓐ something expensive or costly

   Ⓑ something that makes life easier

   Ⓒ a drawing that shows how something works

   Ⓓ made up of many, many parts

2. Before erasers were invented, people fixed a mistake by _____ .

   Ⓐ copying the whole paper over

   Ⓑ rubbing a hole where the mistake was

   Ⓒ washing off the pencil marks

   Ⓓ using a piece of rubber

3. Why did Goldman invent the shopping cart?

   Ⓐ He was tired of people's baskets breaking.

   Ⓑ He wanted bigger baskets so people would buy more.

   Ⓒ He was tired of people forgetting to bring their baskets.

   Ⓓ Goldman owned one of the first supermarkets.

4. In this story, *circular* means _____ .

   Ⓐ rubber

   Ⓑ square

   Ⓒ round

   Ⓓ oval

5. Why did Spilsbury invent puzzles?

   Ⓐ He wanted children to learn about different places.

   Ⓑ He wanted to teach children how to draw.

   Ⓒ He liked carving things in wood.

   Ⓓ He attended the World's Fair in 1904.

6. Why is a safety pin better than a straight pin?

    (A) It is not as safe as a straight pin.

    (B) A safety pin is much bigger.

    (C) A straight pin is more expensive.

    (D) People get pricked less often with a safety pin.

7. In this selection, a *patent* is _____ .

    (A) the idea of the inventor

    (B) a person who solves problems

    (C) a colorful wooden map

    (D) a document that protects an idea

8. Who got the patent and made money on the safety pin?

    (A) a woman who gave Hunt some string

    (B) a man who gave Hunt some wire

    (C) Walter Hunt, the inventor of the safety pin

    (D) No one filed for a patent.

9. How did Lipman and Rechendorfer improve the pencil?

_____

_____

_____

_____

10. What do all the inventions you have read about have in common?

_____

_____

_____

_____

Harcourt • Moving Ahead • Intervention Assessment Book

Name _____ **Date** _____

Fill in the circle in front of the word that makes sense in the sentence.

1. Dad lived in New York when he was my _____ .
   ○ edge
   ○ age
   ○ cage

2. I have a flower box on my window _____ .
   ○ ledge
   ○ legs
   ○ led

3. Let's play basketball in the _____ .
   ○ germ
   ○ gym
   ○ ginger

4. What a long neck the _____ has!
   ○ geography
   ○ generate
   ○ giraffe

5. The _____ gives orders in the army.
   ○ generous
   ○ general
   ○ gently

6. Eating good foods will help you have _____ .
   ○ energy
   ○ engine
   ○ stingy

7. Ms. Powell _____ loaned me her lawnmower.
   ○ genius
   ○ gentleman
   ○ generously

8. Carrots and spinach are _____ .
   ○ vegetables
   ○ villagers
   ○ forgetful

Directions: For items 1–8, fill in the circle in front of the correct answer. For items 9–10, write the answer.

1. Gina Ginetti is a _____ .
Ⓐ detective in Cookie Corners
Ⓑ detective in Fudge Corners
Ⓒ sculptor in Fudge Corners
Ⓓ police officer in Cookie Corners

2. Why is the Gentle Giant important?
Ⓐ The Gentle Giant is the name of a famous statue.
Ⓑ The Gentle Giant is a mean, scary dog.
Ⓒ The Gentle Giant is Gina's pet dog.
Ⓓ The Gentle Giant saved the life of the town's founder.

3. Why doesn't Al like Reggie?
Ⓐ Reggie boasts all the time.
Ⓑ Reggie is a better sculptor than Al.
Ⓒ Al is jealous of Reggie.
Ⓓ Gina likes Reggie better than Al.

4. How does Al feel when the statue is unveiled?
Ⓐ surprised and proud
Ⓑ pleased and excited
Ⓒ angry and upset
Ⓓ nervous and guilty

5. People think Reggie is a genius because _____ .
Ⓐ he is very smart
Ⓑ the pigeons flock to the statue
Ⓒ the statue is very lifelike
Ⓓ the mayor said that the town is lucky to have a great sculptor

Harcourt • Moving Ahead • Intervention Assessment Book

6. Why does Gina want to question Reggie?

Ⓐ Gina is a detective.

Ⓑ She knows Al does not lie.

Ⓒ Reggie is a known thief.

Ⓓ Angela told her to question him.

7. Reggie says that he has an alibi. An *alibi* is _____ .

Ⓐ a reason to do something

Ⓑ being guilty

Ⓒ being nervous

Ⓓ an excuse

8. In this story, *fake* means _____ .

Ⓐ not true

Ⓑ sincere

Ⓒ stolen

Ⓓ trusting

9. Name one way Reggie gives himself away.

_____

_____

_____

_____

10. Now that it has been proven that Al is the true sculptor, what do you think the mayor will do?

_____

_____

_____

Name _____ **Date** _____

Fill in the circle in front of the word that makes sense in the sentence.

1. Plants grow best in rich _____ .
   - ○ sail
   - ○ soil
   - ○ sold

2. Our class always _____ putting on plays.
   - ○ enjoys
   - ○ employs
   - ○ annoys

3. My pencil has a sharp _____ .
   - ○ appoint
   - ○ joint
   - ○ point

4. We asked Troy to _____ our reading club.
   - ○ join
   - ○ choice
   - ○ oil

5. I'll be _____ if you can't go with me.
   - ○ discover
   - ○ distance
   - ○ disappointed

6. This fan is so quiet that it is almost _____ .
   - ○ noseless
   - ○ noiseless
   - ○ noisy

7. Everyone was sure of George Washington's _____ to his country.
   - ○ oily
   - ○ loyalty
   - ○ royalty

8. The _____ in the air made my glasses foggy.
   - ○ moisture
   - ○ poisonous
   - ○ boiling

Harcourt • Moving Ahead • Intervention Assessment Book

Lesson 18: *Just Enough Is Plenty*

Directions: For items 1–8, fill in the circle in front of the correct answer. For items 9–10, write the answer.

1. A person who is *thrifty* _____ .
   - (A) spends all his or her money
   - (B) is very poor
   - (C) saves most of his or her money
   - (D) has a lot of money

2. Another way of saying "his savings grew to a generous sum" is _____ .
   - (A) his money grows in the fields
   - (B) he saved a lot of money
   - (C) his dollar bills grew bigger and bigger
   - (D) he added all his money and got the total

3. The farmer's neighbor _____ his boasting.
   - (A) really likes and enjoys
   - (B) buys more land to encourage
   - (C) makes a roguish plan to stop
   - (D) gets bored with

4. So that the farmer will appear to be as rich as his neighbor, he _____ .
   - (A) buys more land
   - (B) buys a fancy car
   - (C) buys a big house
   - (D) sells a big harvest

5. How does the farmer prove to himself that his neighbor has more animals than he has?
   - (A) His friend tells him.
   - (B) He purchases more pigs and hens.
   - (C) He hears loud oinking and clucking.
   - (D) He sneaks into the neighbor's yard.

6. To further tell the farmer that he does not look like a rich man, the neighbor _____ .

   Ⓐ calls the farmer's house a hut

   Ⓑ buys himself a big, fancy house

   Ⓒ tells the farmer to get a new barn

   Ⓓ boasts the way the farmer did

7. In the evening the farmer looks around and decides that he _____ .

   Ⓐ likes his life as it is

   Ⓑ needs more animals and a new barn

   Ⓒ wants a big, fancy house

   Ⓓ won't brag anymore

8. The farmer learns that the extra animals and crops only make him _____ .

   Ⓐ richer

   Ⓑ tired

   Ⓒ happier

   Ⓓ nervous

9. Explain the meaning of the story's title, "Just Enough Is Plenty."

_____

_____

_____

10. What lesson does the farmer in this selection learn?

_____

_____

_____

Harcourt • Moving Ahead • Intervention Assessment Book

Name _____ **Date** _____

Fill in the circle in front of the word that makes sense in the sentence.

1. The _____ of my favorite book is visiting our school.
   - ◯ author
   - ◯ autumn
   - ◯ auction

2. I _____ the ball when Dawn threw it.
   - ◯ coat
   - ◯ kite
   - ◯ caught

3. A large _____ heard the band concert.
   - ◯ audience
   - ◯ auto
   - ◯ awful

4. I was so sleepy that I had to _____ .
   - ◯ yard
   - ◯ yarn
   - ◯ yawn

5. The awards ceremony was held in the _____ .
   - ◯ awkward
   - ◯ auditorium
   - ◯ August

6. The _____ door opens by itself when you walk up to it.
   - ◯ autograph
   - ◯ automatic
   - ◯ awful

7. It is _____ to throw litter in the street.
   - ◯ unlawful
   - ◯ unlabeled
   - ◯ unlikely

8. Mom was _____ after a hard day's work.
   - ◯ expressed
   - ◯ exhausted
   - ◯ explained

Directions: For items 1–8, fill in the circle in front of the correct answer. For items 9–10, write the answer.

1. What crime has the wolf been charged with?
   - Ⓐ attempted kidnapping
   - Ⓑ stealing sheep
   - Ⓒ chasing a grandma and her granddaughter
   - Ⓓ attempted eating

2. Who is in charge of the court?
   - Ⓐ the bailiff
   - Ⓑ the lawyer
   - Ⓒ Judge Bo Peep
   - Ⓓ Red Riding Cap

3. Where does this play take place?
   - Ⓐ Storyland Court
   - Ⓑ Storyland Jail
   - Ⓒ August, some year
   - Ⓓ the wolf's den

4. How does the wolf try to get around the charge?
   - Ⓐ by telling the truth
   - Ⓑ by using flattery
   - Ⓒ by lying to the judge
   - Ⓓ by apologizing

5. When the wolf eats sheep, he likes to have _____ .
   - Ⓐ cranberry sauce
   - Ⓑ mint sauce
   - Ⓒ mustard
   - Ⓓ sweet peas

Harcourt • Moving Ahead • Intervention Assessment Book

6. To prove his innocence, the wolf claims all the following **except** that _____ .

Ⓐ it's the author's fault

Ⓑ he's a victim of circumstances

Ⓒ he wouldn't hurt a flea

Ⓓ the Three Pigs should be asked

7. In this play, *delicious* means _____ .

Ⓐ very tasty

Ⓑ eaten with mint jelly

Ⓒ eaten whole

Ⓓ very hot and spicy

8. The wolf thinks it's over for him when the Three Pigs are called as witnesses because _____ .

Ⓐ he tried to blow their houses down

Ⓑ he tried to have them for dinner

Ⓒ Bo Peep wants her sheep found

Ⓓ the wolf's mother says he's not bad

9. Why does the wolf say that he and Bo Peep are both victims of circumstances?

_____

_____

_____

10. When is eating considered to be acceptable and not a crime?

_____

_____

_____

Fill in the circle in front of the word that makes sense in the sentence.

1. My brother and I will _____ dinner tonight.
   - ◯ cook
   - ◯ took
   - ◯ look

2. We made a playhouse from scrap _____ .
   - ◯ stood
   - ◯ good
   - ◯ wood

3. I _____ spend more time with my little sister.
   - ◯ shed
   - ◯ should
   - ◯ showed

4. The horse has injured its _____ .
   - ◯ half
   - ◯ hive
   - ◯ hoof

5. I wish I _____ Japanese.
   - ◯ understood
   - ◯ undersea
   - ◯ underpass

6. Be on the _____ for a lost kitten.
   - ◯ strikeout
   - ◯ cookout
   - ◯ lookout

7. The coach kept score in a _____ .
   - ◯ notice
   - ◯ notebook
   - ◯ nothing

8. I petted the sheep's _____ back.
   - ◯ woolly
   - ◯ woody
   - ◯ wavy

Harcourt • Moving Ahead • Intervention Assessment Book

A Clever Plan

Directions: For items 1–8, fill in the circle in front of the correct answer. For items 9–10, write the answer.

1. The Kingdom of Woodlandia is a good place to live for all the following reasons **except** that _____ .
   Ⓐ there is plenty of food
   Ⓑ there is enough firewood
   Ⓒ King Roger is very kind and caring
   Ⓓ the king's ideas are not always the best

2. It isn't smart for every person in the kingdom to have shoes exactly like the king's, because _____ .
   Ⓐ the king has very big feet
   Ⓑ everyone doesn't have the same size foot
   Ⓒ it would take the shoemaker too long to make the shoes
   Ⓓ the people do not like the style of the shoes

3. The second decree King Roger makes is that _____ .
   Ⓐ everyone must have a robe like his
   Ⓑ all coats must have a satin hood
   Ⓒ everyone must have a pet tiger
   Ⓓ everyone needs a pet lion

4. In this selection, *plentifully* means _____ .
   Ⓐ having a good supply of something
   Ⓑ asking for something over and over
   Ⓒ having famine
   Ⓓ not having enough of something

5. In this selection, a *province* is _____ .
   Ⓐ a strange country   Ⓑ an area of a country
   Ⓒ a large city   Ⓓ a big forest

6. A *billion* is equal to a _____ .

    (A) hundred million

    (B) hundred thousand

    (C) thousand million

    (D) trillion

7. The Mayor of Woodlandia tries to solve the problem of the robes by _____ .

    (A) calling together the people and asking their opinion

    (B) meeting with the ministers for each province

    (C) telling the king *no*

    (D) ordering the Woodlandians to make fine robes

8. How does King Roger feel when his subjects appear in the "fine robes"?

    (A) He is angry that they disobeyed him.

    (B) He orders all the people to jail.

    (C) He issues a decree that everyone has to wear grapes and twigs.

    (D) He laughs so hard that he cries.

9. Why can't the Woodlandians follow the king's orders and dress like him?

_____

_____

_____

10. How does the king show his thankfulness to the Woodlandians for pointing out that his idea does not work?

_____

_____

_____

Harcourt • Moving Ahead • Intervention Assessment Book

Fill in the circle in front of the word that makes sense in the sentence.

1. Cowboys protect their feet by wearing _____ .

- ○ boats
- ○ boots
- ○ bats

2. The game will begin very _____ .

- ○ soon
- ○ son
- ○ sun

3. The sky is a bright _____ today.

- ○ bloom
- ○ blow
- ○ blue

4. I drink orange _____ with my breakfast.

- ○ just
- ○ jest
- ○ juice

5. My parents read the _____ every day.

- ○ newspaper
- ○ newborn
- ○ newsboy

6. I packed my _____ for my trip to Grandma's.

- ○ soothing
- ○ suitcase
- ○ suitable

7. We decorated our _____ for Parents' Day.

- ○ scolding
- ○ schoolroom
- ○ scale

8. This gum is too hard to be _____ .

- ○ choose
- ○ chosen
- ○ chewable

Directions: For items 1–8, fill in the circle in front of the correct answer. For items 9–10, write the answer.

1. Forest rangers think that fires improve the forests in all the following ways **except** that the fires _____ .
   - Ⓐ burn old branches
   - Ⓑ burn diseased trees
   - Ⓒ help make the soil richer
   - Ⓓ can cost millions of dollars

2. Which of the following statements is an opinion?
   - Ⓐ Not all forest fires are bad.
   - Ⓑ Firefighters' gear includes fireproof coats and gloves.
   - Ⓒ Airplanes are used to drop chemicals on forest fires.
   - Ⓓ Rain is the best firefighter of all.

3. Fires started by lightning deep in the forest sometimes _____ .
   - Ⓐ cause thunder
   - Ⓑ burn out on their own
   - Ⓒ can be used as campfires
   - Ⓓ don't need watching

4. Which of the following statements is a fact?
   - Ⓐ Forest fires can be exciting and colorful.
   - Ⓑ Fighting fires is a fun job for volunteers, rangers, and pilots.
   - Ⓒ In 1988, there were fires at Yellowstone National Park.
   - Ⓓ Lightning is beautiful in the night sky.

5. In this selection, *volunteers* are people who _____ .
   - Ⓐ get paid to fight fires
   - Ⓑ set fires in the forest
   - Ⓒ aren't paid, but help during big fires
   - Ⓓ drive the fire trucks or fly the planes

Harcourt • Moving Ahead • Intervention Assessment Book

6. If a fire *rekindled,* it _____ .
   - Ⓐ has been put out completely
   - Ⓑ started to burn again after it seemed to be out
   - Ⓒ burned everything in the area
   - Ⓓ was caused by strong wind

7. One of the _____ firefighters face is deciding when to fight a fire and when to let it burn.
   - Ⓐ challenges
   - Ⓑ volunteers
   - Ⓒ curfews
   - Ⓓ loyalties

8. Even though millions of trees were lost in the Yellowstone National Park fire, the forest itself was not lost, because _____ .
   - Ⓐ by the next year grass and flowers began to grow
   - Ⓑ no animals or people were injured
   - Ⓒ there wasn't much snow in the winter and the ground was dry
   - Ⓓ rangers were able to plant new trees and bushes

9. Why should people try to prevent forest fires?

   _____

   _____

   _____

10. Why do firefighters feel that wind is an enemy to fighting forest fires?

   _____

   _____

   _____

Fill in the oval in front of the word that makes sense in the sentence.

1. My shoelace has a _____ in it.
- ○ knot
- ○ know
- ○ knife

5. Computers have taken the place of many _____ .
- ○ tiptoes
- ○ typical
- ○ typewriters

2. A swarm of _____ bothered us at our picnic.
- ○ nights
- ○ nets
- ○ gnats

6. The crew searched for the _____ on the ocean floor.
- ○ shipwreck
- ○ shipshape
- ○ shipyard

3. I scraped my _____ when I raised the window.
- ○ knuckle
- ○ nickel
- ○ knack

7. My _____ says it's almost noon.
- ○ wrinkle
- ○ restroom
- ○ wristwatch

4. The mouse tried to _____ a hole in the wall.
- ○ know
- ○ gnaw
- ○ new

8. The _____ came off when I turned it.
- ○ doorstop
- ○ doorknob
- ○ doorway

Harcourt • Moving Ahead • Intervention Assessment Book

A Place of New Beginnings

Directions: For items 1–8, fill in the circle in front of the correct answer. For items 9–10, write the answer.

1. The setting of this selection is _____ .
   Ⓐ an art museum
   Ⓑ Ellis Island
   Ⓒ New York City
   Ⓓ a doctor's office

2. Why is Ellis Island an important place?
   Ⓐ It's a big island in New York Harbor.
   Ⓑ Many people were married there.
   Ⓒ Many people entering the United States landed there.
   Ⓓ There is a wonderful tour for visitors to the island.

3. After they tour the Baggage Room, Karen and her father go to the _____ .
   Ⓐ Registry Room   Ⓑ Reception Room
   Ⓒ Flag Room   Ⓓ Document Room

4. Before people can qualify for citizenship in the United States, they _____ .
   Ⓐ have to see an examiner
   Ⓑ must take an oath of allegiance
   Ⓒ must have many shots
   Ⓓ must see a doctor

5. Why are immigrants with diseases sent back to their own country?
   Ⓐ So they can spread the diseases at home.
   Ⓑ So they won't bring the diseases here.
   Ⓒ There are better doctors in other countries.
   Ⓓ Americans want to catch all the strange diseases.

6. In this selection, to *take an oath* means to _____ .

Ⓐ celebrate a tradition

Ⓑ stand in line

Ⓒ gain citizenship

Ⓓ make a formal promise

7. It is harder to trace women immigrants than men because women _____ .

Ⓐ do not keep good records

Ⓑ often marry and change their last names

Ⓒ use their original last names now

Ⓓ did not register when they entered the country

8. Karen and her father learn that the Wall of Honor is a list of _____ .

Ⓐ all the people who have ever come here through Ellis Island

Ⓑ the names of people who left the United States

Ⓒ many of the people who came here through Ellis Island

Ⓓ soldiers who fought in World War II for the United States

9. How do you think people felt when they had to leave all their belongings in the Baggage Room at Ellis Island?

_____

_____

_____

10. What do Karen and her father plan to do for Poppa Joe?

_____

_____

_____

Harcourt • Moving Ahead • Intervention Assessment Book

Name _____ **Date** _____

Fill in the circle in front of the word that makes sense in the sentence.

1. Phil's funny jokes make me
   _____ .
   - ○ lack
   - ○ laugh
   - ○ lap

2. The meat was too _____ to
   chew.
   - ○ tuck
   - ○ tug
   - ○ tough

3. Mom says my sister talks on the
   _____ too much.
   - ○ television
   - ○ telegraph
   - ○ telephone

4. Everyone looks blurry in the
   _____ I took.
   - ○ phone
   - ○ photo
   - ○ phrase

5. Josh collects _____ of baseball
   players.
   - ○ autographs
   - ○ alphabets
   - ○ elephants

6. I have been _____ because I
   am sick.
   - ○ cawing
   - ○ causing
   - ○ coughing

7. We get medicine from a
   _____ .
   - ○ physical
   - ○ pharmacy
   - ○ phrase

8. My _____ class is studying
   places in China.
   - ○ geography
   - ○ photography
   - ○ paragraph

Harcourt • Moving Ahead • Intervention Assessment Book

Desert Animals

Directions: For items 1–8, fill in the circle in front of the correct answer. For items 9–10, write the answer.

1. The setting for this selection is the _____ .
   - (A) desert in the daytime
   - (B) desert at night
   - (C) country during the day
   - (D) country at nighttime

2. Many animals of the desert live underground, because _____ .
   - (A) there is more food and water underground
   - (B) it is warmer underground
   - (C) it is cooler underground
   - (D) they want to protect their eyes from the sun

3. Which desert animal keeps its baby underground in a long tunnel?
   - (A) a beetle
   - (B) a digger bee
   - (C) a digger ant
   - (D) a bumblebee

4. The zebra-tailed lizard sometimes runs on its back feet because it _____ .
   - (A) might burn its front feet and body on the hot sand
   - (B) has hurt its back legs
   - (C) has hurt its front legs
   - (D) wants to keep its back legs off the hot sand

5. One kind of slow-moving reptile looks like a _____ .
   - (A) baby turtle
   - (B) land-dwelling turtle
   - (C) small lizard
   - (D) digger bee

Harcourt • Moving Ahead • Intervention Assessment Book

6. The roadrunner runs quickly along the ground, but _____ .

   Ⓐ it can also fly

   Ⓑ it won't eat snakes

   Ⓒ it can sneak up on animals

   Ⓓ it also digs burrows

7. When an old cactus dies from _____, it becomes a home for many animals.

   Ⓐ fire

   Ⓑ disease

   Ⓒ animals eating it

   Ⓓ too much sun

8. Why is it hard to see many animals in the desert during the day?

   Ⓐ Not many animals live in the desert.

   Ⓑ Most animals come out only at night.

   Ⓒ They are too fast to be seen.

   Ⓓ They are hiding from the buzzards.

9. How does the size of the jackrabbit's ears help it?

_____

_____

_____

_____

10. How is the hummingbird like a helicopter?

_____

_____

_____

Name _____ **Date** _____

Fill in the circle in front of the word that makes sense in the sentence.

1. I fixed the hole in my shirt with a needle and _____ .
   - ○ three
   - ○ threat
   - ○ thread

2. You have to hold your _____ when you swim underwater.
   - ○ breath
   - ○ bread
   - ○ break

3. We are expecting stormy _____ tomorrow.
   - ○ wetter
   - ○ weather
   - ○ wheat

4. I'll _____ the ribbon with a ruler.
   - ○ measure
   - ○ meadow
   - ○ meaning

5. A big _____ in the newspaper told about the election.
   - ○ headscarf
   - ○ headline
   - ○ head-on

6. There is a fairy tale about the _____ man and the fox.
   - ○ widespread
   - ○ overhead
   - ○ gingerbread

7. The clouds are _____ to dump rain on our picnic.
   - ○ threatening
   - ○ treating
   - ○ threading

8. I was bored during that _____ movie.
   - ○ dressy
   - ○ dreadful
   - ○ dreamy

Harcourt • Moving Ahead • Intervention Assessment Book

Directions: For items 1–8, fill in the circle in front of the correct answer. For items 9–10, write the answer.

1. Heather has an awful feeling when she wakes up, because _____ .
   (A) her family has just moved to a new house
   (B) she misses her old friends
   (C) it will be her first day at a new school
   (D) it is a cold and dark morning

2. At the beginning of the selection, how does Heather feel about the new school?
   (A) She is excited and eager to go there.
   (B) She thinks she will hate it.
   (C) She knows she'll like her new teacher.
   (D) She knows she won't like the kids.

3. "Heather held her old teacher in *high regard*" means that she _____ .
   (A) thought she was just an average teacher
   (B) missed her old teacher
   (C) loathed her
   (D) admired and respected her

4. Heather thinks about telling her parents that she _____ .
   (A) has a bad headache
   (B) will take the cat with her to school
   (C) doesn't like her mother's cheerfulness
   (D) doesn't want any breakfast

5. Why does Heather decide not to fake a headache?

   (A) She knows trustworthy people don't lie.

   (B) She is afraid her parents will think she is lying.

   (C) She'd just have to go to school the next day.

   (D) She fakes an upset stomach instead.

6. Heather's father is _____ .

   (A) nervous and funny   (B) funny and friendly

   (C) friendly and serious   (D) cheerful and trustworthy

7. In this selection, a *custom* is _____ .

   (A) a person's bad habit

   (B) something someone has never done before

   (C) something someone does out of habit

   (D) a tradition followed in a particular country

8. The neighbor walking her dog turns out to be _____ .

   (A) the driver of Heather's school bus

   (B) the principal at Heather's new school

   (C) Heather's new teacher

   (D) a friendly woman

9. Do you think Heather will like her new school? Why?

_____

_____

10. How do you think Mrs. Weatherbee knows that Heather will be going to her school?

_____

_____

Harcourt • Moving Ahead • Intervention Assessment Book

Name _____ **Date** _____

Fill in the circle in front of the word that makes sense in the sentence.

1. My dog _____ 35 pounds.
   - ○ waves
   - ○ wades
   - ○ weighs

2. Trucks haul _____ across the country.
   - ○ freight
   - ○ fright
   - ○ fret

3. Dad grilled a _____ for dinner.
   - ○ steep
   - ○ stick
   - ○ steak

4. I pulled on the _____ to stop the horse.
   - ○ rinse
   - ○ reins
   - ○ runs

5. Friendly people live in my _____ .
   - ○ neighborhood
   - ○ neighborly
   - ○ neighbors

6. Be careful not to drop that _____ glass.
   - ○ breakdown
   - ○ breakable
   - ○ breathless

7. The number after 17 is _____ .
   - ○ eighteen
   - ○ eight
   - ○ eighty

8. Lincoln is famous for his _____ as President.
   - ○ neatness
   - ○ lateness
   - ○ greatness

**Directions: For items 1–8, fill in the circle in front of the correct answer.
For items 9–10, write the answer.**

1. Who is telling this story?

  Ⓐ Roberto Aguas, Sr.

  Ⓑ Roberto Aguas, Jr.

  Ⓒ Roberto's mother

  Ⓓ Roberto's grandparents

2. Mexican culture is important to Junior and his sister because _____ .

  Ⓐ they are proud of their Mexican heritage

  Ⓑ their grandparents are from Mexico

  Ⓒ their cousins live in Mexico

  Ⓓ for part of the year, Junior and his family visit Mexico

3. What did Junior's grandmother teach him and his sister during
her visit?

  Ⓐ how to grind corn

  Ⓑ how to eat tortillas

  Ⓒ how to make pancakes

  Ⓓ how to make tortillas

4. The family ate the tortillas with all the following **except** _____ .

  Ⓐ corn   Ⓑ salsa

  Ⓒ chile   Ⓓ beans

5. When Junior says that everyone complimented them on their cooking,
he means _____ .

  Ⓐ their relatives didn't like the tortillas he made

  Ⓑ their relatives told them the food was delicious

  Ⓒ everyone thought food from a Mexican restaurant was better

  Ⓓ the food needed more chile pepper

Harcourt • Moving Ahead • Intervention Assessment Book

6. In this selection, *memories* are _____ .
- Ⓐ the same as relatives
- Ⓑ things that will happen soon
- Ⓒ things remembered from the past
- Ⓓ festive parties

7. Relatives include all of the following **except** _____ .
- Ⓐ aunts
- Ⓑ uncles
- Ⓒ cousins
- Ⓓ neighbors

8. In this selection, the *surface* of the table is _____ .
- Ⓐ each of the four legs
- Ⓑ the top of the table
- Ⓒ a special tablecloth
- Ⓓ the side of the table

9. Name the steps involved in making tortillas.

_____

_____

_____

_____

10. Briefly tell what happens at a fiesta.

_____

_____

_____

_____

Harcourt • Moving Ahead • Intervention Assessment Book

Name _____ **Date** _____

Fill in the circle in front of the word that makes sense in the sentence.

1. Our teacher helps us spell words
   _____ .
   - ⃝ correctly
   - ⃝ correcting
   - ⃝ correctable

2. Dawn is very _____ about
   playing any game.
   - ⃝ avoidable
   - ⃝ movable
   - ⃝ agreeable

3. During the long play, I was
   _____ and couldn't sit still.
   - ⃝ restless
   - ⃝ resting
   - ⃝ rested

4. My shirt is dirty, so I'm glad it's
   _____ .
   - ⃝ washer
   - ⃝ washable
   - ⃝ washed

5. I can fill my _____ water bottle
   and drink from it again.
   - ⃝ using
   - ⃝ reusable
   - ⃝ useless

6. The kitten pawed _____ at the
   ball of yarn.
   - ⃝ playfully
   - ⃝ players
   - ⃝ playable

7. I missed two questions on the test
   because of _____ .
   - ⃝ caring
   - ⃝ carefully
   - ⃝ carelessness

8. Some people _____ use more
   water than they need.
   - ⃝ wasted
   - ⃝ wasting
   - ⃝ wastefully

Harcourt • Moving Ahead • Intervention Assessment Book

The West Beckons

Directions: For items 1–8, fill in the circle in front of the correct answer. For items 9–10, write the answer.

1. In this story, *fares* are _____ .
  Ⓐ rivers to cross
  Ⓑ ships
  Ⓒ money charged to riders
  Ⓓ wagons

2. James Marshall hoped to _____ in California.
  Ⓐ find his family
  Ⓑ start a farm
  Ⓒ open a store
  Ⓓ make a lot of money

3. Marshall and John Sutter started a _____ .
  Ⓐ mining business
  Ⓑ wagon train
  Ⓒ railroad business
  Ⓓ sawmill business

4. Marshall made a discovery that started _____ .
  Ⓐ a gold rush
  Ⓑ a wagon train trip
  Ⓒ a war
  Ⓓ a bank

5. What was a result of Marshall's discovery?
  Ⓐ Streams of people rushed to California.
  Ⓑ Marshall got rich.
  Ⓒ Marshall built many sawmills.
  Ⓓ Few people came to California.

6. *Sailors abandoned their ships* means _____ .

  Ⓐ sailors tried to sail their ships faster

  Ⓑ sailors went off and left their ships

  Ⓒ sailors lost their way

  Ⓓ sailors repaired their ships

7. Only a few people who looked for gold _____ .

  Ⓐ stayed poor

  Ⓑ stayed in California

  Ⓒ became rich

  Ⓓ helped settle the land

8. Because of the settlers, California became a _____ state.

  Ⓐ small

  Ⓑ unpopular

  Ⓒ multicultural

  Ⓓ far-away

9. Why is James Marshall still remembered?

_____

_____

_____

_____

10. Why is "The West Beckons" a good title for this story?

_____

_____

_____

_____

Harcourt • Moving Ahead • Intervention Assessment Book

Name _____ **Date** _____

Fill in the circle in front of the word that makes sense in the sentence.

1. The bird flew right _____ my open window.
   - ○ three
   - ○ through
   - ○ throw

2. The bread _____ will need to rise for an hour.
   - ○ do
   - ○ dough
   - ○ dew

3. We have _____ food to last just one day.
   - ○ enough
   - ○ enroll
   - ○ enormous

4. Amanda has _____ her new neighbor to school.
   - ○ brought
   - ○ bring
   - ○ bright

5. I can walk on hot sand because of the _____ of my feet.
   - ○ softness
   - ○ timeless
   - ○ toughness

6. I'll go down the slide _____ I'm a little scared.
   - ○ always
   - ○ although
   - ○ altogether

7. There are exciting chapters _____ this book.
   - ○ thought
   - ○ though
   - ○ throughout

8. I'm sorry that my _____ hurt your feelings.
   - ○ through
   - ○ thoughtlessness
   - ○ thoroughly

Directions: For items 1–8, fill in the circle in front of the correct answer. For items 9–10, write the answer.

1. The very first Americans believed the mountain now called Pikes Peak _____ .
   - (A) was an awful place
   - (B) offered special drinking water
   - (C) kept their world in harmony
   - (D) was something they must climb

2. What difficulty did Pike meet when he and his crew tried to climb to the top of the mountain?
   - (A) The men thought they could do it in a day.
   - (B) It was summer, but it started snowing.
   - (C) Pike's crew became tired and quit.
   - (D) Pike's crew made it to the top, but he didn't.

3. The event that most changed the mountain was _____ .
   - (A) Stephen Long's making it to the top
   - (B) mapmakers naming it Pikes Peak
   - (C) Pike's failing to make it to the top
   - (D) the discovery of gold in the mountain

4. Most of the people who dreamed of getting rich from mining gold _____ .
   - (A) lost everything they had
   - (B) bought mining equipment
   - (C) found that the gold had run out
   - (D) fulfilled their dreams

5. In this selection, *hoisted* means _____ .
   - (A) lowered to the ground
   - (B) moved something along level ground
   - (C) lifted something up the mountain
   - (D) very heavy

Harcourt • Moving Ahead • Intervention Assessment Book

6. When Pike wrote in his *journal,* he was writing _____ .

Ⓐ for a newspaper

Ⓑ for a magazine

Ⓒ a book

Ⓓ in his diary

7. "The mountain was left with holes and gashes." *Gashes* means _____ .

Ⓐ deep cuts

Ⓑ big trees

Ⓒ large rocks

Ⓓ deep rivers

8. After the gold rush, people visited Pikes Peak _____ .

Ⓐ looking for new friends

Ⓑ looking for a new beginning

Ⓒ looking for other ways to the West

Ⓓ to become pioneers

9. Over the years the mountain changed in many ways, but it also remained the same. What is one thing that stayed the same?

_____

_____

_____

10. How did the mountain inspire Katharine Lee Bates?

_____

_____

_____

Harcourt • Moving Ahead • Intervention Assessment Book

Name _____ **Date** _____

Fill in the circle in front of the word that makes sense in the sentence.

1. It's _____ when you don't play by the rules.
   - ○ unwritten
   - ○ unmade
   - ○ unfair

2. I lost my report and had to _____ it.
   - ○ rewrite
   - ○ rerun
   - ○ repay

3. Summer weather can be hot and _____ .
   - ○ discontented
   - ○ disappearing
   - ○ disagreeable

4. Mom says I should never be _____ to anyone.
   - ○ improvement
   - ○ impolite
   - ○ important

5. The _____ train goes straight to the city.
   - ○ nonstop
   - ○ nonsense
   - ○ nonfiction

6. We voted to _____ our club meetings for the summer.
   - ○ dishonor
   - ○ discontinue
   - ○ disconnect

7. The museum has a collection of _____ fossils.
   - ○ preview
   - ○ preschool
   - ○ prehistoric

8. My new invention looks good, but it is _____ .
   - ○ impractical
   - ○ impersonal
   - ○ impatient

Harcourt • Moving Ahead • Intervention Assessment Book

Lesson 28: *An American Legend*

An American Legend

Directions: For items 1–8, fill in the circle in front of the correct answer. For items 9–10, write the answer.

1. Pecos Bill decides it is time for him to leave Texas because _____ .
  Ⓐ there are too many problems in Texas
  Ⓑ there is a stampede of mosquitoes
  Ⓒ Texas is no longer a challenge for him
  Ⓓ he wants to visit the West

2. When Pecos Bill goes out West, he plans to _____ .
  Ⓐ set up a new ranch
  Ⓑ invent a rattlesnake sandwich
  Ⓒ ride a wildcat
  Ⓓ drive out the mosquitoes

3. To Pecos Bill, a real cowhand is all the following **except** _____ .
  Ⓐ rough
  Ⓑ impolite
  Ⓒ untamed
  Ⓓ agreeable

4. A rattlesnake of *impossible* size is one that is _____ .
  Ⓐ very small
  Ⓑ regular-sized
  Ⓒ beyond all belief
  Ⓓ rather large

5. The wildcat does not meet with tragedy because Bill needs _____ .
  Ⓐ a sandwich for lunch
  Ⓑ something to ride
  Ⓒ a meek kitten
  Ⓓ a place for his saddle

---

6. What does Bill use for a napkin to wipe his chin?

Ⓐ the sleeve of his shirt

Ⓑ the beard of a cowpoke

Ⓒ a prickly pear cactus

Ⓓ the wildcat's tail

7. In this selection, *a ration of grub* means _____ .

Ⓐ a pile of bugs

Ⓑ a big meal

Ⓒ swirling clouds of mosquitoes

Ⓓ boiling coffee

8. Bill asks, "Who's boss around here?" The cowpokes reply, _____ .

Ⓐ "We don't have one."

Ⓑ "This is a fateful moment."

Ⓒ "We can start a ranch called Arizona."

Ⓓ "You are!"

9. Name two things Pecos Bill does to repay Texas for all that it did for him.

_____

_____

_____

_____

10. Name two qualities found in this selection that make it a tall tale.

_____

_____

_____

_____

Harcourt • Moving Ahead • Intervention Assessment Book

Name _____ **Date** _____

Fill in the circle in front of the word that makes sense in the sentence.

1. The river is dirty because of
   _____ .
   ○ lotion
   ○ pollution
   ○ vacation

2. The city council's ruling on
   vacant lots was not a
   popular _____ .
   ○ decision
   ○ vision
   ○ possession

3. Winter is _____ time for bears.
   ○ hibernation
   ○ nation
   ○ station

4. I had a long _____ with my
   grandpa about his childhood.
   ○ action
   ○ inaction
   ○ conversation

5. Keisha spoke _____ about how
   much her teachers had helped
   her.
   ○ emotionally
   ○ exceptionally
   ○ nationally

6. I would never _____ leave my
   schoolwork at home.
   ○ internationally
   ○ intentionally
   ○ invention

7. The building that was destroyed
   by the storm is now under
   _____ .
   ○ reservation
   ○ reinventing
   ○ reconstruction

8. We painted new posters as part of
   our classroom's _____ .
   ○ redecoration
   ○ rereading
   ○ rewriting

Harcourt • Moving Ahead • Intervention Assessment Book

Directions: For items 1–8, fill in the circle in front of the correct answer. For items 9–10, write the answer.

1. The brown bat loves to eat _____ .
   - Ⓐ spiders
   - Ⓑ bats
   - Ⓒ mosquitoes
   - Ⓓ beetles

2. How does the brown bat locate its victims?
   - Ⓐ Mosquitoes like boggy marshes.
   - Ⓑ Its screeches bounce off its victims.
   - Ⓒ Mosquitoes fly onto its wings and stick there.
   - Ⓓ The brown bat eats almost half its weight in one night.

3. A bolas spider is different from other spiders because it _____ .
   - Ⓐ spins a web to catch bugs
   - Ⓑ uses its tongue to catch bugs
   - Ⓒ doesn't catch bugs
   - Ⓓ makes a bolas to catch bugs

4. When a moth is nearby, the bolas spider can _____ .
   - Ⓐ see it
   - Ⓑ feel it
   - Ⓒ hear it
   - Ⓓ taste it

5. One way a praying mantis catches bugs is to _____ .
   - Ⓐ sit still, watch, and pounce
   - Ⓑ pray
   - Ⓒ fly around at night
   - Ⓓ spin a web

Harcourt • Moving Ahead • Intervention Assessment Book

6. "A praying mantis's front legs are like steel traps" means that they are _____ .

Ⓐ very short

Ⓑ very weak

Ⓒ very long

Ⓓ very strong

7. Carnivorous creatures are _____ .

Ⓐ vegetarians

Ⓑ flesh-eating animals

Ⓒ flying in

Ⓓ chocolate-covered ants

8. How is the girl like the bug-catching creatures in the selection?

Ⓐ They all catch bugs.

Ⓑ They all let bugs go.

Ⓒ They all eat bugs.

Ⓓ They all reduce the insect population.

9. How does a bolas spider keep food until it's hungry?

_____

_____

_____

_____

10. Write one sentence that tells the main idea of this selection.

_____

_____

_____

_____

Name _____ **Date** _____

Fill in the circle in front of the word that makes sense in the sentence.

1. I'd love to take a long vacation during the _____ .
   - ○ summer
   - ○ sometime
   - ○ summary

2. We buy fresh vegetables at the _____ .
   - ○ marker
   - ○ marvelous
   - ○ market

3. We found a _____ ear of corn in our garden.
   - ○ perform
   - ○ perfect
   - ○ person

4. Our class will present a _____ about our school's history.
   - ○ profit
   - ○ progress
   - ○ program

5. _____ , there are 200 students in our school.
   - ○ Alphabet
   - ○ Altogether
   - ○ Although

6. We will _____ the cookies, three to a bag, before the bake sale.
   - ○ prepackage
   - ○ prevent
   - ○ president

7. The campers took their own water into the _____ .
   - ○ wildlife
   - ○ wilderness
   - ○ wildly

8. My parents _____ to go along on the class trip.
   - ○ volcanic
   - ○ volume
   - ○ volunteered

Harcourt • Moving Ahead • Intervention Assessment Book

Lesson 30: *Air Force Kids*

Directions: For items 1–8, fill in the circle in front of the correct answer. For items 9–10, write the answer.

1. What do Paul and Ricardo have in common?
   Ⓐ Both live on Air Force bases.
   Ⓑ Ricardo is curious about Alaska.
   Ⓒ Paul is moving to Spain.
   Ⓓ Both boys have lived in many places.

2. In Spain, Ricardo sees _____ in the village.
   Ⓐ a moose
   Ⓑ farm animals
   Ⓒ interesting animals
   Ⓓ snowshoes

3. In what country has Paul never lived?
   Ⓐ Turkey   Ⓑ Germany
   Ⓒ Spain   Ⓓ the United States

4. Ricardo says he will be *cautious* if he meets a moose, which means that he will be _____ .
   Ⓐ brave
   Ⓑ scared
   Ⓒ careful
   Ⓓ intrigued

5. A good way to settle differences between people is to _____ .
   Ⓐ compare outcomes
   Ⓑ be cautious
   Ⓒ argue
   Ⓓ compromise

6. Ricardo is pleased because his move to California has been postponed. Now he will be able _____ .

Ⓐ to learn about California

Ⓑ to play against the World Cup soccer team

Ⓒ to have Paul as a friend for a year

Ⓓ to visit places in Spain he has not seen

7. Before Ricardo moves to California, he wants to learn about _____ .

Ⓐ baseball

Ⓑ basketball

Ⓒ soccer

Ⓓ football

8. When Paul moves to Spain, _____ .

Ⓐ he thinks he will miss Alaska

Ⓑ it will be his first time out of the United States

Ⓒ he will not live on an Air Force base

Ⓓ Ricardo will be in California

9. From photos that Paul sends, what does Ricardo decide about Air Force base schools?

_____

_____

_____

10. How do you know that Ricardo likes soccer?

_____

_____

_____

Harcourt • Moving Ahead • Intervention Assessment Book

Answer Key

....

Gram's Plant Parade		
page 1	**page 2**	**page 3**
1. van	1. C	6. B
2. plane	2. A	7. B
3. frame	3. A	8. B
4. parade	4. D	9. He learns to enjoy planting.
5. landscape	5. C	10. She will plant bulbs there.
6. classmates		
7. flagpole		
8. made		

Click!		
page 4	**page 5**	**page 6**
1. bill	1. A	6. C
2. lid	2. C	7. D
3. hide	3. B	8. B
4. win	4. A	9. She takes Mike's picture.
5. hillside	5. B	10. The word *click* appears in red on the page.
6. willing		
7. inside		
8. spilling		

A Troublesome Nose		
page 7	**page 8**	**page 9**
1. slope	1. A	6. C
2. nod	2. B	7. B
3. spot	3. C	8. A
4. hope	4. D	9. Possible response: It's the story of a fox, a dog, and a frog visiting a tropical land for the holidays. Troublesome problems arise.
5. stroking	5. D	
6. robin		10. the troublesome nose
7. smoking		
8. jogging		

Joe DiMaggio, One of Baseball's Greatest		
page 10	**page 11**	**page 12**
1. beak	1. B	6. A
2. seeds	2. A	7. B
3. stream	3. C	8. C
4. key	4. B	9. Accept any logical response. Possible responses: He hit 46 home runs in one season. He's in the Baseball Hall of Fame.
5. seaweed	5. C	
6. selling		10. Possible response: He could hit and had speed, but more importantly he was a good sportsman.
7. resting		
8. endless		

Answer Key

Amelia's Flying Lesson

page 13	page 14	page 15
1. scrub	1. A	6. A
2. stung	2. B	7. B
3. truck	3. D	8. C
4. junk	4. C	9. Possible response: June changes more. At the beginning of the story, she is afraid to go down the slide. At the end, she wants to fly, too.
5. useful	5. C	
6. accuse		10. Possible responses: Yes, because using it would be fun. No, because someone could get hurt on it.
7. unplugged		
8. shutting		

Can-Do Kid

page 16	page 17	page 18
1. mall	1. B	6. B
2. salt	2. C	7. C
3. fall	3. C	8. B
4. tall	4. A	9. Possible response: People stop to listen to Walt sing, and then they go to the CD stall.
5. baseball	5. D	
6. sidewalk		10. Possible response: because Walt can do what he says he will do
7. install		
8. talking		

Small but Brave

page 19	page 20	page 21
1. wags	1. D	6. D
2. rain	2. A	7. D
3. stay	3. B	8. B
4. trail	4. C	9. Possible response: Loyal fights with the fox that is trying to get the hens. The fox bites his leg.
5. explain	5. D	
6. payment		10. Possible response: Loyal learns that it is important to be brave, but it is better to have a best friend.
7. subway		
8. waiter		

Bringing Back the Puffins

page 22	page 23	page 24
1. cheer	1. B	6. D
2. path	2. D	7. A
3. wishes	3. A	8. D
4. Thank	4. C	9. Possible response: that the puffins would instinctively return to Egg Rock to breed and raise their young
5. sunshine	5. A	
6. bathtub		10. Accept any two: being eaten by seagulls, caught in fishing nets, or harmed by big waves
7. exchange		
8. fisherman		

Harcourt • Moving Ahead • Intervention Assessment Book

Answer Key

....

Green Tomatoes

page 25	**page 26**	**page 27**
1. part	1. B	6. A
2. yard	2. A	7. B
3. art	3. D	8. C
4. hard	4. A	9. Nick didn't think he could take money for green tomatoes.
5. argument	5. C	10. Carla's pickles
6. farmyard		
7. carpet		
8. large		

A Day with the Orangutans

page 28	**page 29**	**page 30**
1. soak	1. B	6. B
2. toast	2. A	7. A
3. owns	3. C	8. D
4. coach	4. D	9. Possible response: The baby will need to build a nest everyday as an adult orangutan.
5. raincoat	5. C	10. Possible response: so that the orangutans will have a place to make their homes
6. snowballs		
7. rowboat		
8. approach		

A Home on the Oregon Trail

page 31	**page 32**	**page 33**
1. storm	1. C	6. C
2. roar	2. B	7. D
3. floor	3. D	8. B
4. pour	4. A	9. Possible response: In Baltimore she wasn't lonely, because she could visit with the neighbors who lived nearby. She is lonely in the West, because there are no neighbors. She misses the ocean.
5. yourself	5. D	10. Possible response: The fire had been bad, but meeting Patrick had been nice.
6. important		
7. doorway		
8. seashore		

Sisters Forever

page 34	**page 35**	**page 36**
1. heard	1. B	6. B
2. word	2. C	7. D
3. nurse	3. B	8. A
4. dirty	4. A	9. She judges LaVerne to be uninterested in sports because LaVerne has long hair and collects stuffed animals; no.
5. perfect	5. B	10. LaVerne thinks the girls will be friends after all.
6. birthday		
7. thirteen		
8. purple		

Answer Key

Oak Grove Picnic

page 37	**page 38**	**page 39**
1. ideas	1. B	6. C
2. title	2. D	7. B
3. museum	3. A	8. D
4. sky	4. C	9. Before the owls leave, the animals have to be watchful, because the owls might eat them.
5. recently	5. A	10. The summer has been dry, and food has become scarce. When acorns ripen, animals can get enough food to eat and to store for the winter.
6. ladybug		
7. tomato		
8. university		

A Pen Pal in Vietnam

page 40	**page 41**	**page 42**
1. pie	1. C	6. A
2. tight	2. C	7. B
3. flight	3. D	8. D
4. tie	4. A	9. Accept any three: Some people live in small towns; there are farms; people eat rice; people ride in boats; both countries have large cities; people eat meat broth; bicycles are common; people dress much the same way in the two countries.
5. lighthouse	5. B	10. Possible response: Michelle and her mother will fly to Ho Chi Minh City. Mrs. Tran's brother will meet them. They will meet Kim at the market.
6. highway		
7. frightening		
8. Fireflies		

Wolf Pack: Sounds and Signals

page 43	**page 44**	**page 45**
1. loud	1. C	6. B
2. power	2. B	7. C
3. crown	3. D	8. A
4. found	4. A	9. Possible responses: licking the alpha wolf's muzzle, holding another animal's snout, wagging their tails
5. outside	5. D	10. Accept any logical response.
6. Cowboys		
7. somehow		
8. underground		

Harcourt • Moving Ahead • Intervention Assessment Book

Answer Key

Who Invented This?

page 46	page 47	page 48
1. cents	1. B	6. D
2. fancy	2. D	7. D
3. decide	3. B	8. B
4. tricycle	4. C	9. They invented erasers that were attached to the pencils.
5. cereal	5. A	10. They solve a problem and make life easier.
6. peacefully		
7. celebrate		
8. certainly		

The Case of the Strange Sculptor

page 49	page 50	page 51
1. age	1. B	6. B
2. ledge	2. D	7. D
3. gym	3. A	8. A
4. giraffe	4. C	9. Accept one: Reggie says he doesn't know where Al lives. He also mentions that the statue was in Al's basement.
5. general	5. C	10. Accept any logical response.
6. energy		
7. generously		
8. vegetables		

Just Enough Is Plenty

page 52	page 53	page 54
1. soil	1. C	6. A
2. enjoys	2. B	7. A
3. point	3. C	8. B
4. join	4. A	9. Possible response: More wealth means more work. Having just enough is nice.
5. disappointed	5. D	10. Possible response: Be happy with what you have.
6. noiseless		
7. loyalty		
8. moisture		

Big Bad Wolf and the Law

page 55	page 56	page 57
1. author	1. D	6. D
2. caught	2. C	7. A
3. audience	3. A	8. A
4. yawn	4. B	9. Possible response: In stories about them, Bo Peep is always dressed in a ruffled dress and bonnet, while the wolf always eats other animals.
5. auditorium	5. B	10. as long as the eating involves food and not animals or people
6. automatic		
7. unlawful		
8. exhausted		

Answer Key

• •

A Clever Plan

page 58	**page 59**	**page 60**
1. cook	1. D	6. C
2. wood	2. B	7. B
3. should	3. C	8. D
4. hoof	4. A	9. Possible response: They do not have the silks, satins, or jewels that he owns.
5. understood	5. B	
6. lookout		10. Possible response: He puts on a large royal picnic for everyone.
7. notebook		
8. woolly		

Fire in the Forest

page 61	**page 62**	**page 63**
1. boots	1. D	6. B
2. soon	2. A	7. A
3. blue	3. B	8. A
4. juice	4. C	9. Possible response: Fires can put people and their homes in danger.
5. newspaper	5. C	
6. suitcase		10. Possible response: The wind can change so quickly that it can whip up flames in many directions. It's something the firefighters can't control.
7. schoolroom		
8. chewable		

A Place of New Beginnings

page 64	**page 65**	**page 66**
1. knot	1. B	6. D
2. gnats	2. C	7. B
3. knuckle	3. A	8. C
4. gnaw	4. A	9. Possible response: They must have feared that they would never see their belongings again.
5. typewriters	5. B	
6. shipwreck		10. get Poppa Joe's name added to the wall
7. wristwatch		
8. doorknob		

Desert Animals

page 67	**page 68**	**page 69**
1. laugh	1. A	6. A
2. tough	2. C	7. B
3. telephone	3. B	8. B
4. photo	4. A	9. Possible response: The size of the ears keeps the jackrabbit from getting too hot, because the extra skin allows the animal to let off more heat.
5. autographs	5. B	
6. coughing		10. Possible response: A hummingbird can hover in one spot and can fly backward just like a helicopter.
7. pharmacy		
8. geography		

Harcourt • Moving Ahead • Intervention Assessment Book

Answer Key

<table>
<tr><td colspan="3" align="center">School Days</td></tr>
<tr>
<td valign="top">

page 70
1. thread
2. breath
3. weather
4. measure
5. headline
6. gingerbread
7. threatening
8. dreadful

</td>
<td valign="top">

page 71
1. C
2. B
3. D
4. A
5. A

</td>
<td valign="top">

page 72
6. B
7. D
8. C
9. yes, because her teacher is friendly and Heather is starting to feel better even before she leaves home
10. Heather's parents probably told her when they were talking before breakfast.

</td>
</tr>
</table>

<table>
<tr><td colspan="3" align="center">When I Was Eight</td></tr>
<tr>
<td valign="top">

page 73
1. weighs
2. freight
3. steak
4. reins
5. neighborhood
6. breakable
7. eighteen
8. greatness

</td>
<td valign="top">

page 74
1. B
2. A
3. D
4. A
5. B

</td>
<td valign="top">

page 75
6. C
7. D
8. B
9. Possible response: First, you mix the batter. Next, you shape the batter into little balls. Then, you roll it out.
10. People at a fiesta sing, dance, and eat lots of good food.

</td>
</tr>
</table>

<table>
<tr><td colspan="3" align="center">The West Beckons</td></tr>
<tr>
<td valign="top">

page 76
1. correctly
2. agreeable
3. restless
4. washable
5. reusable
6. playfully
7. carelessness
8. wastefully

</td>
<td valign="top">

page 77
1. C
2. D
3. D
4. A
5. A

</td>
<td valign="top">

page 78
6. B
7. C
8. C
9. Possible response: Marshall discovered gold in California, which led to an important event in American history.
10. Possible response: Many people wanted to go to California during the gold rush, and travelers from around the world still go there.

</td>
</tr>
</table>

<table>
<tr><td colspan="3" align="center">Purple Mountain Majesty</td></tr>
<tr>
<td valign="top">

page 79
1. through
2. dough
3. enough
4. brought
5. toughness
6. although
7. throughout
8. thoughtlessness

</td>
<td valign="top">

page 80
1. C
2. B
3. D
4. A
5. C

</td>
<td valign="top">

page 81
6. D
7. A
8. B
9. Possible response: It remained a place of hope and dreams.
10. She wrote the words for "America the Beautiful."

</td>
</tr>
</table>

Answer Key

An American Legend

page 82
1. unfair
2. rewrite
3. disagreeable
4. impolite
5. nonstop
6. discontinue
7. prehistoric
8. impractical

page 83
1. C
2. A
3. D
4. C
5. B

page 84
6. C
7. B
8. D
9. Accept any two: He holds the first roundup, invents the lariat and other gadgets, and tames tornadoes.
10. Possible response: Events and animals are greatly exaggerated. The story has many funny incidents.

Bug Catchers

page 85
1. pollution
2. decision
3. hibernation
4. conversation
5. emotionally
6. intentionally
7. reconstruction
8. redecoration

page 86
1. C
2. B
3. D
4. B
5. A

page 87
6. D
7. B
8. A
9. Possible response: The spider wraps a moth in silk and hangs it up until the spider is hungry.
10. Some creatures have amazing ways of catching bugs.

Air Force Kids

page 88
1. summer
2. market
3. perfect
4. program
5. Altogether
6. prepackage
7. wilderness
8. volunteered

page 89
1. A
2. B
3. D
4. C
5. D

page 90
6. C
7. A
8. B
9. The schools are probably pretty much alike everywhere around the world.
10. He tells about the soccer game and signs his letter "Your soccer friend."

Harcourt • Moving Ahead • Intervention Assessment Book

Student's Name _____

Lesson/Selection	Pupil Score (Circle the number correct.)	Date	Comments
1. Gram's Plant Parade short vowel /a/; long vowel /ā/a-e vocabulary/selection comprehension	1 2 3 4 5 6 7 8 1 2 3 4 5 6 7 8 9 10		
2. Click! short vowel /i/; long vowel /ī/i-e vocabulary/selection comprehension	1 2 3 4 5 6 7 8 1 2 3 4 5 6 7 8 9 10		
3. A Troublesome Nose short vowel /o/; long vowel /ō/o-e vocabulary/selection comprehension	1 2 3 4 5 6 7 8 1 2 3 4 5 6 7 8 9 10		
4. Joe DiMaggio short vowel /e/; long vowel /ē/ee, ea, ey vocabulary/selection comprehension	1 2 3 4 5 6 7 8 1 2 3 4 5 6 7 8 9 10		
5. Amelia's Flying Lesson short vowel /u/; long vowel /(y)o͞o/u-e vocabulary/selection comprehension	1 2 3 4 5 6 7 8 1 2 3 4 5 6 7 8 9 10		
6. Can-Do Kid vowel variant /ôl/al, all vocabulary/selection comprehension	1 2 3 4 5 6 7 8 1 2 3 4 5 6 7 8 9 10		
7. Small but Brave short vowel /a/; long vowel /ā/ai, ay vocabulary/selection comprehension	1 2 3 4 5 6 7 8 1 2 3 4 5 6 7 8 9 10		

Lesson/Selection	Pupil Score (Circle the number correct.)	Date	Comments
8. Bringing Back the Puffins consonant digraphs /sh/sh, /ch/ch, tch, /th/th vocabulary/selection comprehension	1 2 3 4 5 6 7 8 1 2 3 4 5 6 7 8 9 10		
9. Green Tomatoes R-controlled vowel /är/ar vocabulary/selection comprehension	1 2 3 4 5 6 7 8 1 2 3 4 5 6 7 8 9 10		
10. A Day with the Orangutans long vowel /ō/oa, ow vocabulary/selection comprehension	1 2 3 4 5 6 7 8 1 2 3 4 5 6 7 8 9 10		
11. A Home on the Oregon Trail R-controlled vowels /ôr/or, oor, ore, oar, our vocabulary/selection comprehension	1 2 3 4 5 6 7 8 1 2 3 4 5 6 7 8 9 10		
12. Sisters Forever R-controlled vowels /ûr/er, ear, ur, or, ir vocabulary/selection comprehension	1 2 3 4 5 6 7 8 1 2 3 4 5 6 7 8 9 10		
13. Oak Grove Picnic long vowels /ā/a; /ē/e, y; /ī/i, y; /ō/o; /yōō/u vocabulary/selection comprehension	1 2 3 4 5 6 7 8 1 2 3 4 5 6 7 8 9 10		
14. A Pen Pal in Vietnam long vowel /ī/igh, ie vocabulary/selection comprehension	1 2 3 4 5 6 7 8 1 2 3 4 5 6 7 8 9 10		
15. Wolf Pack: Sounds and Signals vowel diphthongs /ou/ou, ow vocabulary/selection comprehension	1 2 3 4 5 6 7 8 1 2 3 4 5 6 7 8 9 10		

Student's Name _____

Lesson/Selection	Pupil Score (Circle the number correct.)	Date	Comments
16. Who Invented This? consonant /s/c vocabulary/selection comprehension	1 2 3 4 5 6 7 8 1 2 3 4 5 6 7 8 9 10		
17. The Case of the Strange Sculptor consonant /j/g, dge vocabulary/selection comprehension	1 2 3 4 5 6 7 8 1 2 3 4 5 6 7 8 9 10		
18. Just Enough Is Plenty vowel diphthongs /oi/oi, oy vocabulary/selection comprehension	1 2 3 4 5 6 7 8 1 2 3 4 5 6 7 8 9 10		
19. Big Bad Wolf and the Law vowel variants /ô/aw, au(gh) vocabulary/selection comprehension	1 2 3 4 5 6 7 8 1 2 3 4 5 6 7 8 9 10		
20. A Clever Plan vowel variants /o͝o/oo, ou vocabulary/selection comprehension	1 2 3 4 5 6 7 8 1 2 3 4 5 6 7 8 9 10		
21. Fire in the Forest vowel variants /o͞o/oo, ue, ui, ew vocabulary/selection comprehension	1 2 3 4 5 6 7 8 1 2 3 4 5 6 7 8 9 10		
22. A Place of New Beginnings consonant digraphs /n/kn, gn; /r/wr vocabulary/selection comprehension	1 2 3 4 5 6 7 8 1 2 3 4 5 6 7 8 9 10		

Lesson/Selection	Pupil Score (Circle the number correct.)	Date	Comments
23. Desert Animals consonant digraphs /f/ph, gh vocabulary/selection comprehension	1 2 3 4 5 6 7 8 1 2 3 4 5 6 7 8 9 10		
24. School Days short vowel /e/ea vocabulary/selection comprehension	1 2 3 4 5 6 7 8 1 2 3 4 5 6 7 8 9 10		
25. When I Was Eight long vowel /ā/ea, ei, eigh vocabulary/selection comprehension	1 2 3 4 5 6 7 8 1 2 3 4 5 6 7 8 9 10		
26. The West Beckons suffixes: -ly, -ful, -able, -less vocabulary/selection comprehension	1 2 3 4 5 6 7 8 1 2 3 4 5 6 7 8 9 10		
27. Purple Mountain Majesty letter pattern *ough* vocabulary/selection comprehension	1 2 3 4 5 6 7 8 1 2 3 4 5 6 7 8 9 10		
28. An American Legend prefixes: un-, re-, dis-, im-, non-, pre- vocabulary/selection comprehension	1 2 3 4 5 6 7 8 1 2 3 4 5 6 7 8 9 10		
29. Bug Catchers suffixes -tion, -sion vocabulary/selection comprehension	1 2 3 4 5 6 7 8 1 2 3 4 5 6 7 8 9 10		
30. Air Force Kids review syllable patterns vocabulary/selection comprehension	1 2 3 4 5 6 7 8 1 2 3 4 5 6 7 8 9 10		

Harcourt • Intervention Assessment Book